SAXON SUPERMAN

About the Author

Linda Hague, an East Anglian born and bred, left the region briefly to take a degree at London Universty, then returned to teach history in a Cambridge school. She now lives in Hereward country – close to Ely – with her husband, her daughter and a great many cats.

SAXON SUPERMAN
The Story of Hereward
by Linda Hague

Anglia Young Books

First published in 1989
by Anglia Young Books
Durhams Farmhouse, Ickleton
Saffron Walden, Essex CB10 1SR

© 1989 Linda Hague

All rights reserved. No part of this publication
may be reproduced, stored in a retrieval system, or
transmitted in any form or by any means, electronic,
mechanical, photocopying, recording or otherwise
without the written permission of the Publisher.

Illustrations by Edward Blake

Design and production in association with
Book Production Consultants
47 Norfolk Street
Cambridge CB1 2LE

British Library Cataloguing in Publication Data
Hague, Linda
  Saxon superman.
  I. Title
  823'.914 [J]

ISBN 1-871173-04-3

Typeset in 11/15 point Palatino by Witwell Ltd, Southport
and printed in Great Britain by
Redwood Burn Ltd, Trowbridge, Wiltshire

AUTHOR'S NOTE

Even now, nearly 900 years after his death, Hereward is remembered throughout East Anglia as a hero. But was he really a hero – or just an attractive villain?

The story of Hereward is full of daring exploits, scandals and battles and it is often impossible to separate the legends about him from the facts. But he certainly did exist and will never be forgotten.

Some people believed that Hereward was the son of the famous Lady Godiva (the one who rode naked through the streets of Coventry) but this is not so. A pity; she would have been a fitting mother for the daredevil Hereward!

We know that, for much of his life, Hereward had a faithful servant called Martin Lightfoot. So, in this book, Martin tells the story – a story that combines fact and legend.

I hope you will enjoy it.

CHAPTER ONE

My name is Martin Lightfoot and, for as long as I can remember, my life has been bound up with the life of Hereward.

In the early days, I was a young servant in the household of Leofric, a landowner, and his wife, Ediva. They lived on the edge of the fenlands, in a small market town called Bourne, in Lincolnshire.

Hereward was their son and, even as a youngster, he was impossible to ignore. Somehow, he always made sure he was noticed. Usually by causing trouble!

Hereward grew up into a stocky, well built, handsome young man with piercing eyes. He had a strong personality and a quick temper, from which I often suffered in later years! He was always keen to prove his strength and he enjoyed wrestling, fighting and hunting.

But there was another side to his character. He could be very charming and sensitive and was an accomplished musician. I often heard him playing the harp to entertain a lady friend!

However, few people knew about this quieter Hereward. All they saw was a wild young man who disrupted the life of Bourne by causing quarrels and fights.

His poor father, Leofric, embarrassed by constant complaints from the neighbours and thoroughly fed up with Hereward for spending so much family money, warned him time and again to behave himself. But, of course, Hereward took no notice.

The last straw was when Hereward got into trouble with the law over some land. I didn't understand all the details, but it meant that he had to leave Bourne. Just before he left he came to me:
'I need a good servant, Martin,' he said. 'Someone I can trust. I want you to come with me. You must groom my horse, clean my weapons, and help me fight my enemies.'

I stared at him, open-mouthed. I had never been out of Bourne in my life. He smiled:
'I am going to see the world, Martin. This is a great chance for you. Are you man enough to come with me?'

I squared my shoulders:
'I'm your man, sir. You can depend on me!'

I was young and easily influenced by Hereward's charm. My life would have been a lot easier if I had not so readily made that promise to him. But I can't honestly say that I regret making it. My life has certainly never been dull!

And so it was that, on a bleak cold morning, we set out at dawn for Scotland to begin our new life. As the houses of Bourne became small dots in the distance, I turned round several times for a last look at the place I had loved all my life. But Hereward never looked back.

At that time, Scotland was ruled by Hereward's godfather, Gilbert, and it was in his house that we made our new home. Hereward took to life in Scotland with great enthusiasm. He went hawking and hunting and enjoyed life to the full, never, apparently, giving any thought to his family in Bourne and the trouble he had caused them.

On the way back from a hawking expedition one day, Hereward and I both heard some terrible shouts and screams coming from his godfather's courtyard. We galloped towards the noise and soon saw that a ferocious bear had escaped from a menagerie of wild animals. It was attacking everything in sight. It had already savaged a horse and two dogs and it was now advancing on a young girl who was cowering in terror as the bear got closer and closer. I was too frightened to move, but Hereward tried to urge his horse foward. The poor beast refused to go, so Hereward leapt off, drew his sword, and rushed, shouting, into the courtyard. As I watched, the bear turned and lumbered towards him. It rose on its hind legs and prepared to attack. Hereward was doomed. I could watch no more and I closed my eyes.

An ear-splitting yell from Hereward brought me to my senses and I rushed forward in time to see the huge bear reel back and crash to the ground with Hereward's sword firmly embedded in its skull.

What rejoicing followed! Hereward was proclaimed a champion and a hero, and naturally, he had a lot of attention from the Scottish girls. Hereward revelled in all this but it wasn't long before the local men became very jealous. So jealous, in fact, that a gang of them attacked Hereward, intending to get rid of this handsome imposter for ever. But their plan went wrong and Hereward killed three of his attackers instead.

This, of course, could not be tolerated, and we were soon forced to leave Scotland – rather quickly!

· · · · ·

After a long and tedious journey, we ended up in Cornwall, and I was hoping for a rest. But I should have known better!

Hereward was soon involved with a Pictish giant and a beautiful princess. Against her will, the princess had been promised in marriage to the giant, but she hated him and desperately loved an Irish prince. Hereward gallantly vowed to free the princess and fight the giant.

The giant was huge and heavy, but Hereward, although much smaller, was quick on his feet and, in the end, outwitted the giant and killed him.

A hero again, he was presented with a magic sword as a reward. But, as before, he managed to arouse the anger and jealousy of the local people and so – once more – we made a fast escape.

• • • • •

This time we set sail for Ireland to search for the Irish prince loved by the Cornish princess. When Hereward had told me he was going to see the world, he had really meant it!

Hereward was involved in many battles in Ireland and I was constantly amazed by his courage, daredevil tactics and leadership. In the end, he found the Irish prince and we returned to Cornwall to re-unite the couple. I'm glad to say that, as far as I know, they lived happily ever after.

Shortly after the wedding, Hereward heard that his father had died.

'Martin,' he said, 'we must go home.'

I was very sad to hear of the old master's death, but I longed to see Bourne again and so it was with a cheerful heart that I made the preparations for our journey. We would sail all along the south coast of England, then up the east coast and in through The

Wash and down the rivers to Lincolnshire. It would be a long journey but easier than going by land – or this is what we thought.

But fate decreed that I should not see Bourne again for some time. Our ship hit a terrible storm and we were blown off course and shipwrecked on the coast of Flanders.

My spirits were very low and I longed even more for my home, but Hereward wanted adventure so, instead of making plans to return to England, we stayed on in Flanders.

Hereward fought in several expeditions for the Count of Flanders and gained even greater fame as a brilliant soldier. Here, too, he won his famous horse, Swallow, the ugliest horse in the world – but also the fastest!

I didn't think Hereward would ever settle down and get married, but in Flanders he met the beautiful Torfrida and she became his wife. Torfrida was not only beautiful, she was also kind and understanding, although many people believed her to be a witch. She certainly put a magic spell on Hereward and they were very happy together.

Hereward seemed quite content to live a peaceful life in Flanders and I was only too happy to enjoy a lazy, quiet time for once. But I should have known that it wouldn't last.

One day, news came that the Normans had conquered England.

This news shattered our peace for ever.

CHAPTER TWO

'Martin!'

Hereward's voice boomed into the darkness. As I struggled to get up, still dazed by sleep, I thought, 'What now?' I soon found out.

'We are going to England. Just you and I – to spy out the land. I'll go mad if I don't find out what those Normans are doing. Pack quickly, Martin.'

And Hereward strode out.

Poor Torfrida sobbed most of the night and eventually cried herself to sleep, knowing that she could do nothing to stop Hereward walking into more trouble.

So, we left the next day, on a longship, and for once we had an uneventful journey. Acquiring some horses, we approached the outskirts of Bourne at nightfall a week or so later. As we rode slowly along the streets in the dark, we noticed that all the doors and windows were tightly closed. No-one was about and all around us we sensed fear. This was not the Bourne we knew.

It was vital we found somewhere safe to stay and we

went at once to the house of Surturbrand, a loyal friend.

Hereward was uneasy. He said we mustn't tell anyone who he was until we knew exactly what was happening. So, having decided on a plan, we cautiously approached the house. We knocked quietly and heard furtive movements inside. Slowly, the wicker window was opened and a frightened face peered out.

'Have no fear,' whispered Hereward. 'I am a nobleman from Flanders and need shelter for the night. Please hide us from the Normans.'

The door opened and we hurried inside.

'Quick man,' said a voice. 'Bring the horses through the house and tie them up at the back.'

So, for the moment, we were safe. But not for long! In this house, Hereward heard of the disastrous events which had occurred in England and to his family. As we listened, I could see the anger on his face and realised we were in for more trouble.

We were told that the King, Edward the Confessor, had died in 1066 without an heir and the people of England, naturally anxious to have a leader, persuaded Harold Godwinson to rule, although the terrifying sight of a comet passing through the sky almost made him change his mind.

So, Harold had been crowned King. But William of Normandy claimed that *he* had been promised the throne of England. He refused to accept that Harold was King, so, in 1066, he had invaded England.

A large Norman army had landed at Pevensey Bay in Sussex and they were greatly surprised to find no opposition – no Saxons waiting to attack!

When Hereward heard this, he was furious and demanded a reason. He was told that King Harold and the Saxons had been forced to march north to Yorkshire to fight the Vikings, who had launched an attack. So, it was not until he had defeated the Vikings at Stamford Bridge, that King Harold heard of the Norman invasion.

Immediately, without any rest, King Harold and the Saxons marched south to deal with William. There had been a great battle on 14th October 1066 – the Battle of Hastings. King Harold had been killed and William had claimed England by Right of Conquest. He had been crowned King on Christmas Day 1066, and immediately there had been a tragedy. Crowds outside Westminster Abbey had been cheering, but the Norman guards had thought that the noise was a riot and they had burned the houses, fearing William was in danger.

Hearing all this, Hereward leapt to his feet in a rage, and I had to stop him rushing immediately from the house, brandishing his sword. Eventually he calmed down and listened, with increasing horror, to the rest of the news.

The Normans had apparently been busy ever since, building wooden castles to defend themselves from the Saxons, who were not happy with their new rulers. William wanted complete control, and he had organised soldiers to seize the manors and treasures of families who opposed him. As we sat there, we learned of the dreadful events in Bourne – which had happened only the day before. A party of Normans had arrived at Hereward's home, demanding treasure. His younger brother had been at home and he had fought heroically to defend his mother, killing two of the attackers. But he had been hopelessly outnumbered and the Normans had cut off his head, mounting it on a spike above the Manor gate.

At this, Hereward leapt from his stool, with hatred in his eyes. He stood and shook and then he grabbed me roughly by the shoulder:
'Revenge, Martin,' he said. 'I must have revenge!'

In no time Hereward's armour and helmet were disguised under a woman's black cloak and we were creeping towards the sound of Norman merriment and celebration, coming from his father's hall. As we approached under the ghostly moonlight, Hereward vowed to kill them all. His anger mounted as we passed his father's serfs cowering in their huts like frightened rabbits. At the gate we paused and looked up. I shall never forget the dreadful sight that met our eyes. Hereward's brother's head was above the gate. Hereward stumbled towards it, removed the head and, wrapping it in his cloak, he kissed the cold forehead and placed the bundle gently on the ground. Completely calm, but filled with cold fury, Hereward made his way to an unshuttered window. I followed like a shadow and together we peered into the hall, ablaze with candlelight.

The table was laden with food, all served on his father's best silver plate. Ale flowed freely and it was obvious that most of the men and women were quite drunk as they lolled at the table or slept on the floor.

I felt Hereward tremble with anger as he watched the man sitting in his father's chair listening to the minstrel singing rude songs about the English. Then someone spoke of Hereward calling him a rogue and coward who dared not show his face.

Hereward could control himself no longer and, motioning me to stand guard at the door, he ran forward, burst into the hall and, yelling the loudest war cry I have ever heard, he brandished his sword. He quickly cut down the minstrel, then advanced, turning the drunken feast into a terrible scene. Most of the Normans were too drunk to fight and were quite unable to understand the sight that faced them. Many had no weapons and soon ale-cups, knives and benches were flying through the air.

But to no avail. Hereward kept advancing, killing anyone in his way. Those who escaped through the door had me to contend with! The sound of laughing and singing was now replaced by screams and groans. Hereward had killed the Norman's leader and all of his followers. What a gruesome task followed as, one by one, each Norman head was placed where Hereward had found the head of his brother. Hereward's revenge had begun. I could not desert him; my place was beside him whatever happened.

CHAPTER THREE

His anger spent, Hereward came towards me. He carefully picked up his brother's head and again entered the Manor House. Silently I followed and we made our way into the deep shadows at the end of the hall. Here we found Hereward's mother, crouched and trembling; she had witnessed the whole ghastly scene.

Hereward passed me his gruesome bundle and knelt before her. Gradually, she became aware of his presence:
'Hereward,' she cried, and, flinging her arms round him, she sobbed as if she would never stop.

'It's alright mother; I'm here. You're safe now,' said Hereward, gently.

Her terror slowly receded and she began to relax:
'My boy. You are back! You have saved us! Never leave again!'

Hereward bowed his head:
'I must leave again, mother. I have much to do to rid our land of the Normans.'

There was hatred in his voice as he spoke of the people who had caused his mother so much pain.

After much persuasion, she finally agreed to go to Crowland Abbey, a place of safety, while Hereward completed his mission.

Suddenly I became aware of voices outside the Manor and, looking out into the yard I saw, in the weak light of dawn, the people of Bourne, who had been woken by all the noise and had cautiously approached the house to discover what had happened. Hereward also heard them, and slowly we made our way out of the shadows, across the hall and to the door.

A great roar went up from the crowd as Hereward appeared; many were overjoyed to see him. But I realised, too, that many were afraid; afraid of what William the Conqueror would do to them and to their village when he heard of the dreadful events of last night. Raising his arm for silence, Hereward spoke:
'Good people of Bourne; I have restored my own inheritance. These Normans cannot stand against the fury of Saxons!'

An enormous cheer met his words. Then he continued:
'I will return to lead you into victory over the Normans! No Frenchman will be spared.'

Hereward looked around and he realised that not all his listeners were cheering. Some hung their heads and gazed at the ground. He raised his voice and it rang out with confidence:

'Surely no Saxon will be cowardly enough to reject this challenge? Are we all of one mind? Are you with me?'

I watched as, gradually, Hereward's magical personality won over the whole crowd. At last he had them all in the palm of his hand. He promised them victory and the restoration of their homes.

'On my return, I will set fire to what, by right, are my own three hill-top villages. Better this than they should be taken by the accursed Normans. It will be a sign for you that I await your support.'

By now, the crowd's excitement was at its height. They knew they had a brave leader and soon the whole of England would know. I was proud to be Hereward's companion, although I knew that great danger lay ahead.

Before long, we were travelling again. This time, with Hereward's mother, via the inland waterways to Crowland Abbey. The body of Hereward's brother lay in the boat and we rowed silently along the narrow channels, a sombre sight in the early morning. Soon, the Abbey came in view; a large building set on piles of oak driven into the fens. It was a quiet, peaceful place, but Hereward knew that King William had plans to put his own monks into the abbeys of England and, if it happened here, Hereward would lose his land at Rippingdale which belonged to

Crowland Abbey. In this way, people were losing their land all over the country. This made Hereward even more determined to drive out the Normans. But for the present, at least, Hereward was sure that his mother would feel safe here. He settled her with the monks, kissed her fondly, and promised to return.

I followed Hereward as he made his way to the Abbey church and a chill went through me as I heard him make a sacred vow never to rest until his land was safe from the clutches of the Normans.

I was exhausted, but Hereward's command:
'To Peterborough, Martin!' spoken with strength and determination, kept me on my feet. Why were we going there?

We made an easy journey to Peterborough; news of Hereward's exploits had travelled quickly and many Normans had fled in fear.

When we arrived, Hereward spoke with authority:
'I wish to see my old overlord, Abbot Brand,' he said, and we were soon ushered into a cold room in the Abbey where Abbot Brand sat in his chair, well covered with furs and looking frail and ill. However, at the sight of Hereward, he rose from his seat and, stumbling, fell towards him, grasping him for support. His delight was obvious and I thought that we must have come to save the Abbey from the Normans as we had heard that King William was to

replace Abbot Brand, upon his death, with a Norman Abbot, Turold, who would then control the Abbey's land. But I was wrong.

Hereward spoke with reverence to the aged Abbot: 'I wish you to do something for me before I continue the fight,' he said.

'Well boy?' said the old Abbot.

'Make me a knight, my lord Abbot,' said Hereward. 'I have done a deed worthy of a true knight, and as a true knight I wish to lead our land to victory.'

Abbot Brand agreed and the following day we went to the vast Abbey church. Although few were present, the Mass was solemn and impressive. Hereward made his way towards the altar and laid his belt and sword upon it; he knelt humbly at the steps until the Gospel was finished and I watched with awe as the sword, which had been blessed, was placed on his neck. He had been created a knight with God's blessing. The monks, with due solemnity, replaced his belt and sword around his waist. Then we all rose and, as Mass was sung, Hereward looked at peace, filled with an inner strength.

Bidding farewell to the old Abbot and his monks, we set out again for Crowland for a final parting from Hereward's mother. The Abbot received us with a troubled face and I knew that the peace of these few

days was over. It was not long before Hereward was again filled with fury as he learned that the Normans, who were only knighted by their King, had laughed when they heard that Hereward had been knighted by a priest. And a certain Norman, Sir Frederick, had sworn to kill Hereward and place his head on a spike, or capture him and put him in chains. He had his headquarters in an inn at King's Lynn in Norfolk.

I had hardly had time to digest all this before we were flat out, heading for King's Lynn; Hereward was angered beyond measure that *he* should be the cause of laughter – Norman laughter.

We reached King's Lynn and, flinging himself from his horse, sword drawn, Hereward entered the inn and faced Sir Frederick. Quite calmly, he spoke:
'I am Hereward. I heard you wished to see me. As I am a polite and helpful fellow, here I am.'

Then, with lightning speed, he moved forward and cut off Sir Frederick's head. For a moment, there was stunned silence in the room, then, suddenly, there was chaos. Other knights rushed at him, but Hereward slashed with his sword, killing three or four, and emerged quite unharmed. Leaving the inn, he vaulted onto his horse and galloped off. As I sped after him, I wondered wearily where I would end up next!

CHAPTER FOUR

It was to Flanders again.

'At last,' I thought, 'a rest from danger and the fear of Norman attack.'

But we were only returning to collect Torfrida and then make haste back to England. So much for my hopes of a peaceful existence in Flanders; I should have known better. Hereward would not rest until the Normans were defeated.

Torfrida was overjoyed to see Hereward alive and well, but here joy soon vanished when she realised that he had come to take her back to England.

'How can I leave my home, Martin? A strange land awaits me, full of danger.'

However, it was not long before she was packing up her home and her jewels. Like me, she knew Hereward, knew his determination, and knew she had to give him her support.

Soon, we were all on our way back to the fens, a new home for Torfrida. The voyage by sea from Flanders to the Norfolk coast was difficult. The sea was rough and poor Torfrida, when she finally came on deck, looked pale and drawn, feeling seasick as well as homesick. I watched her as she stood on the deck and had her first glimpse of the fens. I could imagine how she felt as she gazed out over the dreary mud creek into which we sailed. As she looked ahead, all that could be seen was a great expanse of flat land stretching for miles into the grey distance. It was cold, and a fierce north-east wind swept the lonely land.

'What have I done, Martin?' she whispered.

But she was brave and I knew that she would stand by Hereward through all danger. Now he had two faithful companions.

'Martin!' Hereward's voiced boomed across at me. 'Go and search the area. See what you can find out and make haste back to us.'

As soon as we landed, I set off, accompanied by two or three others. Within a day, we were back. There was no sign of the Normans in Holbeach, Spalding or Bourne. Our news was received with great celebration and soon we set out, marching forward. We passed men working in the fields who downed tools and followed us. Torfrida was filled with pride when she saw the respect her husband commanded. It was a large band that reached Bourne and immediately Hereward set fire to the three hill-top villages, his promised signal was there for all to see!

As I stood there, watching the flames leap into the sky, I began to believe that Hereward *would* succeed. His boyish troubles were over; he was our leader. Torfrida seemed to be thinking the same. She smiled and pressed Hereward's arm with her hand.

Before long, men poured into Bourne from all over the land. Men dispossessed by the Normans, men related to Harold Godwinson, men related to Hereward – a desperate band, anxious to be led into victory. What a collection assembled there!

I met Wulfric the Blackface, so-called because he once blackened his face with dust and entered the enemy's camp. He told me how he had killed ten of them with his spear. And Wulfric the Heron, nicknamed 'Heron' by the Normans because of his long neck and legs, also kept us entertained with tales of his adventures. He used his long leaping-pole to jump from one patch of safe ground to another in the treacherous fenland bog. No Norman dared to follow him for fear of sinking to his death in the swamp. Wulfric the Heron had lost his manor to the Normans and, by all accounts, he had caused havoc amongst the invaders ever since, once freeing four men about to be hanged on Wroxham Bridge, near Norwich. He had appeared out of the fen, leapt onto the bridge, freed the prisoners and then set about the Normans with his axe, killing them all before leaping to safety. Definitely a man to follow Hereward!

There were many others, including Leofwine the Scythe who, when attacked by twenty people, used his scythe and killed or wounded all of them. There were identical twins called Douti and Outi, both fierce fighters, and Leofwine the Cunning, a man who had never successfully been kept in prison.

Hereward's close friends and relations also arrived and they were quite a collection of vagabonds for Trofrida to meet. His nephews came, his cousin, his chaplain and his cook, and a follower called Winter, who was so short he was almost a dwarf, but he was also immensely strong.

It cannot have been easy for Torfrida to meet all these people and accept them as her husband's loyal followers, but she did, with grace and charm. She was indeed a worthy wife.

So, Hereward had his men, but now he had to turn them into an army and I realised that all his fighting experience overseas had stood him in good stead. My admiration for the man grew every day as I watched him turn this motley band into a well organised fighting force.

Throughout all this preparation, Hereward was waiting for the Danes to arrive. They were a formidable force and they had promised to join Hereward and rid the land of the Normans. But the days dragged on and still they did not arrive.

Hereward began to despair.

It was Torfrida who persuaded him to face his men and tell them of his fears. As I stood and listened, I felt the great comradeship Hereward had bred amongst his followers:
'If you wish to leave now, do so in peace before the Normans surround us,' said Hereward.

'Never! Never!' shouted his men. 'We are with you Hereward. We can save England with or without the help of the Danes.'

But it was not long before we heard news of the Danes' defeat in York. William the Conqueror was victorious and was beginning to stamp his authority all over the land. Each day more and more defeated men arrived to join us. Hereward made his plan:
'We are going to Ely, Martin. It is a place of safety for those who have rebelled against the Normans. We can join with those already there and then, with me as the leader, we can achieve victory.'

His enthusiasm infected us all, including Torfrida, and we set out for Ely.

As we travelled through the fens, I felt sorry for Torfrida. She had endured so much and now she was faced by this vast flat expanse of undrained swamp, through which meandered many small tributaries of the River Ouse. Here and there we passed firm islands rising well above the fen. Some small, with a few huts, like Stuntney, some much larger with land for pasture, like Chatteris. But all around our boats was the wet and soggy marshland in which large pools of black water gleamed ominously in the moonlight.

By dawn we could see the bare skyline and the wild landscape covered with reeds and scrubby bushes. Suddenly the silence was broken by the sound of a coot and we shivered as the mist swirled around us. We were all thinking of our fate should we topple into this black morass and be sucked down into the depths.

As we gazed ahead, a large island appeared in the lightening sky. This island held the settlements of Downham, Witchford, Sutton, Haddenham and Stretham, among others, but it was Ely and its great Abbey, built around the shrine of its founder, Etheldreda, that loomed above them all. What a sight! It dominated the fens and made us fearful as we sat beneath it in our boats, each of us filled with foreboding. What lay ahead of us on this island? Would we really be safe at last?

CHAPTER FIVE

Wearily, we climbed out of the boats onto the island. As we dragged ourselves up the steep slope towards Ely, we began, at last, to feel safe. The height of the island gave a splendid view; no man could approach us without being seen. As I looked out over the swamp surrounding the island, my courage grew. No-one could approach except by boat – an easy target – and if enemies came under cover of darkness they would undoubtedly stray from the firm ground and sink, slowly but surely, into the murky depths. I imagined the Normans trying to make the hazardous journey by boat through unknown territory, sailing through the small channels choked by weeds and moving mudbands, unaware of the danger of heavy rain which would quickly swell the rivers and tributaries, joining them together to form large swirling stretches of water to cover the reeds and fenland and capsize boats with terrifying speed.

Oh yes. I felt safe. Hereward had made the right decision.

I soon found out that the monks of Ely, led by Abbot Thurston, an old friend of King Harold, were surprisingly warlike. They were so frightened that

William would attack and take the Monastery that they welcomed Hereward with open arms and were quite happy for him to make a camp on their island.

'Right men, to work!' shouted Hereward, and before long we were settled into our thatched wooden huts, surrounded by earth ramparts and sheltered by the great Abbey of Ely. Although the huts leaked and were filled with smoke from the open fires in their centres, we were safe. We had no comforts; Torfrida's bed was just a pile of rushes hastily thrown on the hard earth floor. It was cold and miserable, surrounded by the deadly but comforting marshland.

However, the monks were good to us and we spent many happy evenings sharing a good meal with them in their refectory, soldiers and monks sitting side by side. What food we had! Nature was certainly on our side! The swamps, which defended us, also provided us with reeds for thatch and beds, hay for the animals and great supplies of food. The rivers were teeming with fish and the marshes full of eels – a very tasty meal. Wild game abounded and, as the land was so fertile, we were not short of any food crops. There was plenty of ale, too, to wash down our food! We did not fear a siege; we could sit out here for years.

Hereward was delighted by the steady flow of supporters coming to Ely and soon we were joined by the long-awaited Danes, who had failed in their attempt to make Sweyn the king of England. Although Hereward had waited a long time for the Danes, and was disappointed by their defeat by William in York, he was still ready to welcome them. He was willing to join with them to attack the fenland abbeys, about to be taken over by French abbots. The Danes wanted to loot the treasures of the abbeys, but Hereward wanted to stop the abbeys' lands falling into Norman hands.

But there were some people in England who disapproved when Hereward started these attacks; especially when he attacked Peterborough.

Hereward had been knighted in Peterborough. It was a place of great riches and was called 'The Golden Borough'. Hereward was very sad when he heard of the death of his old friend, Abbot Brand. However, we soon heard that his replacement, Abbot Turold, a fierce and warlike monk chosen by King William, was on his way to Peterborough with an armed escort of 160 Norman knights.

Hereward was determined to stop him.

'I will show you the way to the Golden Borough,' cried Hereward to the Danes.

The Danes were delighted. At last they had a chance to get real riches to take back home. Before long, we were leading the Danes through the fens towards their plunder. Many of us wondered if we were doing the right thing, but we knew Hereward; he was so hot-headed and once he had made up his mind that the Normans should not have Peterborough, there was nothing we could do to stop him. So we followed.

The monks knew we were coming and I have heard since that the largest group, who favoured King William, had sent the Sacristan, Yware, laden with as much treasure as he could carry, to meet Abbot Turold and warn him of our approach. But we still got there first, and the war chants of the Danes must have terrified the waiting monks.

As the sun rose over the river, we sailed nearer and nearer. When we landed, we found that the monks had barricaded the gates and doors. We could not get in. The Danes prowled round like angry tigers, impatient for the kill.

'Fire! Set fire to the houses by the gate. We shall enter by fire!' yelled Hereward.

As flames leapt into the sky, destroying the monks' houses and most of the town, Hereward led our marauding band, chanting and shouting, through the Bolhithe Gate. We could feel the heat of the flames on our backs as we surged forward. The Danes didn't care and rushed in, pushing each other into the flames in their haste to get at the treasures.

Total chaos followed. We found the monks, cowering and terrified, kneeling and weeping. The Danes howled like savages, but Hereward protected the monks and sent the Danes to search for the treasure. It was not long before they found where it was hidden and they stole everything they could carry; the jewelled crown from the crucifix, golden crosses, the golden altar-front, silver and jewels, books, money and all the precious treasures hidden in the steeple by the monks. Their bloodcurdling shouts echoed through the building as they rushed out, time and again, their arms laden.

At last we got back to our boats on the River Nene. I looked back and saw the Golden Borough destroyed. Flames and smoke filled the air and then, as the smoke cleared slightly, I saw that only the Abbey and one single house were still standing.

The monks had all fled except one, Leofwine the Long, who was ill and in the infirmary and he was left unharmed. It must have been a sad sight when Abbot Turold finally arrived at the end of that day, long after we had left. We were a subdued group as we made our way back to Ely; even Hereward was quiet. On our return, there was a great meeting and the Danes told us that they were leaving.

'England is lost. We shall take what we have gained from Peterborough and go.'

They had made a secret agreement with William that they would be allowed safe passage home with the treasure, so long as they left immediately. Hereward rose to his feet and we were all quiet as he spoke:
'We are Englishmen. We would rather die here than in another kingdom. We shall remain and continue the fight. We will live and die as Englishmen.'

We all leapt to our feet then and cries rang round the hall:
'Hereward is right!'

'We shall live and die fighting the French!'

'We shall defend our homeland. We shall not run away!'

So, the treasures of Peterborough were loaded onto the Danish ships and they sailed away. We heard that they had been tossed in rough seas during a fierce storm, but did reach land safely.

Once again, we were on our own. Hereward, although blamed by many for such an outrageous attack on Peterborough, maintained that he had agreed to keep Peterborough out of Norman hands. He had none of the treasure; that was scattered all over Scandinavia by now.

We settled down again in Ely. But all of us, including Hereward, were awaiting William's next move. What would he do?

CHAPTER SIX

We didn't have long to wait. As soon as William heard that the Danes had gone, he began to march towards Ely. Hereward remained very calm as news arrived from his spies that a large army was being led by William to Ely. Some were Frenchmen who feared losing their new lands in England and some were men from France and Flanders, hired to fight.

Most of us were tense and on edge, but not Hereward. He kept us all cheeful. However, I began to worry again when I heard that William had made camp on Castle Mound in Cambridge. He was getting very close. Soon he was at Willingham, where firm land reached to within half a mile of Aldreth on the edge of *our* island. But, as Hereward pointed out, that half mile in between us was the fen, and very difficult to cross.

Hereward soon had us building a rampart on the shore of the island, behind which we watched and waited. William and his men made camp outside Willingham on Belsar's Hill. We saw hundreds of men pour down the narrow bridleway carrying timber to make a bridge to cross to Aldreth. We watched as they tried to drive piles down into the fen to make a firm base, and laughed loudly as each attempt failed. Next, they set to work on a floating bridge. Large tree trunks appeared and beams, which lay on animal hides. Slowly, this bridge was pushed out into the fen. I began to get worried; it looked like succeeding! Hereward, however, just smiled:

'Wait and see!' he said.

Every now and then we would set out in our canoes and glide in and out of the reeds, firing arrows at the Normans, just to annoy them. But Hereward gave us strict instructions not to damage the bridge.

Soon it was finished and the area in front of the floating bridge appeared to be moving as hundreds of men prepared to advance over to Aldreth.

'There are so many!' said Torfrida, astonished.

As she spoke, a long column of knights in armour and foot soldiers in leather jerkins made their way slowly to the bridge.

'Let them come,' said Hereward. 'The more the better. They have made a trap for themselves.' We could hear the excitement in his voice.

'Look! Look – there – already!'

The Normans, spurred on by the thought of victory and treasure, began to hurry and to push forward. Men fell off the bridge into the black bog, crying for help, but ignored by the others as they began to run forward.

'Watch comrades!' yelled Hereward and, as we watched, the bridge, unable to hold so many, began to sway and to sink slowly into the fen. The back tilted down and the bridge slipped from the slimy bank at Aldreth.

'You'll have to hurry if you want to reach us, Frenchmen,' cried Hereward.

Already those at the front were faced by black ooze and no bridge. They tried to stop, but those behind continued to surge forward.

'Come on, jump like men!' shouted Hereward, with a cruel laugh.

In a few seconds, those at the front were wallowing waist deep in slimy mud and water. Hereward had been right. The bridge was a complete failure.

Torfrida peered down from our rampart and recoiled in horror as she saw men trampled underfoot, pushed deep down into the bog, forming a bridge of human bodies. Scaling ladders were placed on top of them as their companions tried to climb our ramparts.

'Now!' shouted Hereward, and immediately we started to hurl stones, shoot arrows and fling javelins and

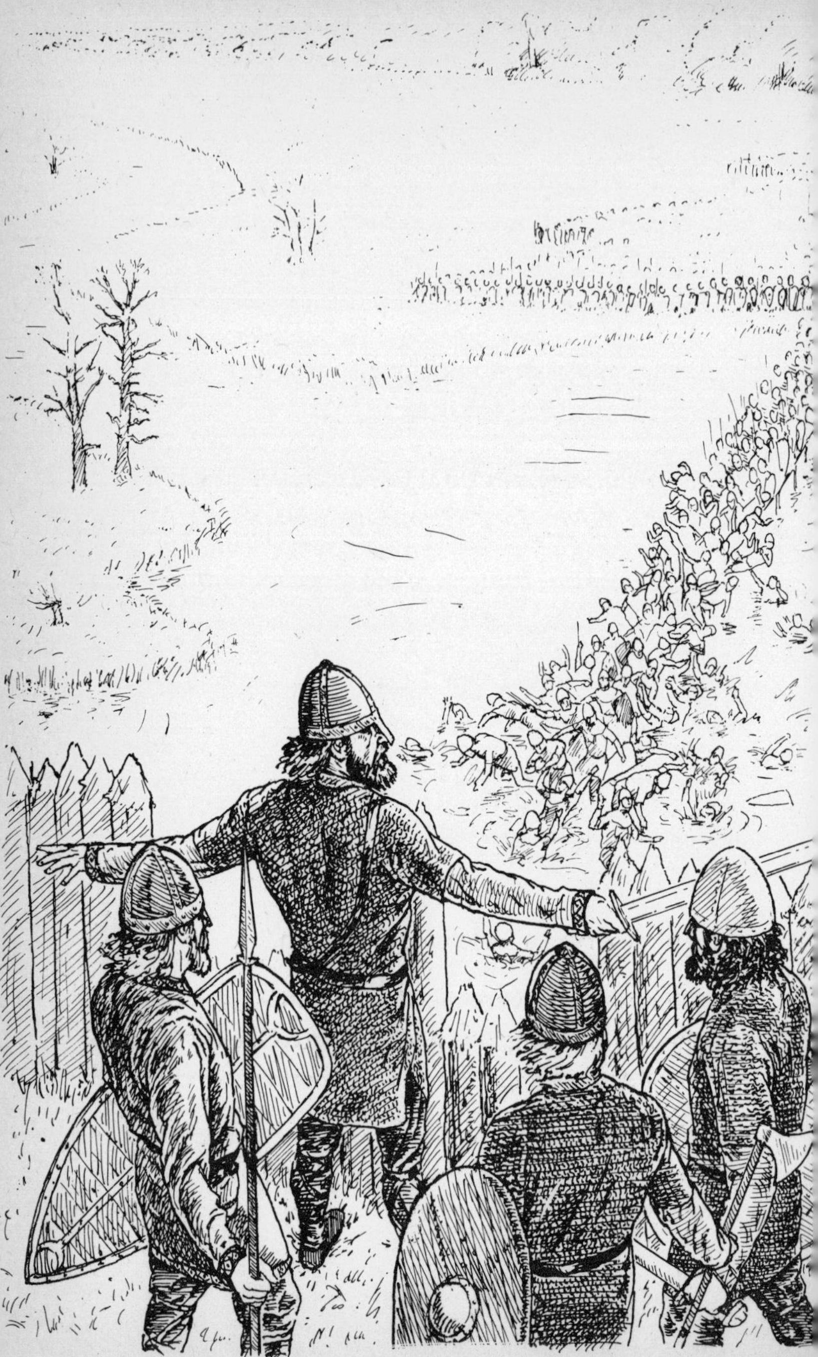

these rained down onto the helpless French, flailing in the murky water. One scaling ladder, heavy with men, was pushed easily away by Hereward, and screams echoed around as men plunged to their deaths. But still they came, man after man, to meet certain death. One Norman knight, Deda, somehow managed to reach the top and thrust Hereward back with a blow from the hilt of his sword. As he clambered over the rampart, he stumbled and fell to his knees, and Hereward recovered.

'Yield!' said Hereward, but Deda raised his sword and crashed it down onto Hereward's helmet.

'Well hit,' yelled Hereward, 'but you cannot harm me. Yield! Why throw away your life?'

Deda looked round, one Norman surrounded by the English, and dropped his sword.

'Wise man,' said Hereward.

Torfrida stepped forward.

'My husband's prisoners are mine, and such a gallant knight deserves a welcome, not death.'

Suddenly, there were piercing screams and yells. We rushed to the ramparts just in time to see the bridge, strained to its limits, topple over sideways and watch hundreds of men become engulfed by the black slime.

'Victory! Victory!' we cried, and when our shouts had

died down there was an eerie hush as we watched our enemies slowly sink and disappear into the fen.

William had failed.

What feasting we had that night! Deda was Hereward's guest and he had been promised a safe journey back to William as long as he swore to report back truthfully how we fared in Ely. Hereward treated him well and that first night he sat in obvious surprise facing the feast in front of him: duck, wild fowl, pike, perch, eels, venison and as much ale as he could drink! He was equally amazed to see the knights and monks sitting side by side at the hall table and, at the high table, the Abbot, earls, Hereward and Torfrida. The noise of voices grew louder as the feast went on, and Deda relaxed, enjoying himself and the company. It was almost dawn before we went to bed, tired but glad that we had shown Deda how well we lived. He would soon see much more to report back to William.

In the weeks which followed, he was shown a lot. He met most of the men on the island and grew to admire them for their courage and determination. He often spoke of his admiration for Hereward:
'I've never met anyone like him,' he said.

Hereward had set out to charm him, and charm him he certainly did. He took Deda on a tour of the island, showing him the abundance of wild fowl and on a hunt, where they took a hundred ducks. He pointed out the woods full of heron.

'I didn't think there were so many in the whole world!' said the astonished Deda.

Deda saw otters, weasels, ermines and pole-cats trapped for fur robes – and fish, so many fish.

'Enough to feed the world for Lent,' he said.

He saw fertile, rich land, producing large quantities of food. He saw the deer park, with red and fallow deer and the woods full of hares and pigs. He joined the expeditions, in narrow flat-bottomed punts, to other islands, protected by the fen, where herds of cattle were fattened for extra food. He was amazed at our skill with the leaping poles and watched as we travelled swiftly and with ease from patch to patch of firm ground. He was also aware of our forays at night, gliding swiftly through the fens, ambushing the Normans when they least expected it, burning villages and hamlets, a constant pressure on them, keeping them on edge for our next move. Hereward had taught us these guerilla tactics well and Deda's admiration for him grew daily.

After about a month, Hereward spoke to him:
'The time has come for you to return to William. Remember your oath. You must give him a full and detailed account of all you have seen.'

'Have no fear, Hereward. The adventures I have had, the hospitality I have received, will all be reported. I arrived on foot, with an empty stomach. I leave well fed, with new clothes and on a horse. William shall know of your strength and power.'

With that he left. Hereward stood and watched him go, his arms folded:
'That will give William plenty to think about, Martin. But now we must prepare ourselves; we do not know what he has been doing this past month. I think it is time a spy was sent to his camp!'

This sounded ominous. Was Hereward about to embark on a final attack, a final effort to gain his revenge? What danger faced us now?

CHAPTER SEVEN

'No, Torfrida, you cannot leave here,' shouted Hereward.

There had been a great argument about who should go as a spy to William's camp. We had all offered – even Torfrida – and we had all begged Hereward not to go himself, but he was determined.

He cut his hair short, put on filthy clothes and left on Swallow.

He was gone several days and we were all getting anxious when he reappeared, jubilant. What a story he had to tell!

After he'd left Ely, Hereward had met a potter and, giving the man a silver penny, he had loaded Swallow with pots; it was the perfect disguise – Hereward the Potter! He rode through Mildenhall calling 'Pots! Pots! Good Pots!' and no-one guessed who he was. He then made haste to Brandon, where he knew William had made camp after his defeat at Aldreth. Slowing down, he became once again the potter and, leading Swallow, made his way towards William's court.

By now it was dusk and he started to look for

lodgings. Just outside the town, he found the perfect place – a hut of mud and turf. A dreadful looking hag answered his knock and agreed to give him a bed for the night in return for a couple of pots. Hereward threw himself down onto the rushes and pretended to sleep. There was something strange about the old hag and he thought, if he kept his ears open, he might learn something from her. He was right!

Later that night, a second old crone arrived and Hereward was certain now that they were both witches. He kept quiet, for even he was afraid of their powers, and listened to their mumblings. He learnt that they had been in touch with his oldest rival in Lincolnshire, Ivo Taillebois! Ivo had given them gold and they were to help William defeat Hereward by sorcery! The first old crone (who he now realised was the Witch of Brandon) had told Ivo that William must build another causeway and attack Hereward again.

The two witches went out of the hut and Hereward followed them into the garden and heard them chanting their strange spells in the moonlight. Soon, he had heard quite enough and he crept back to his bed of rushes.

The next morning, Hereward decided to go to William's court as a potter and see what else he could find out. As he tied up Swallow, the scullions from William's kitchen saw him and called him over, offering him food. His plan was working! He followed them into a large room with an open fire where a huge spit of meat was being turned by a miserable-looking lad. The wooden tables were laden with meat which was being cut up and hung from the ceiling. Herbs hung from the walls and baskets filled with vegetables were piled on the floor.

The people in the room spoke among themselves as they examined the pots and Hereward sat in the corner, ate his food and kept his ears open. He learned that another attack *was* planned and, even as he sat there eating, boats, men and tools were already on their way to Aldreth.

The scullions decided to have sport with Hereward and gave him plenty to drink. He continued to play along and take all their taunts and insults until one of them pulled his beard.

This was too much for Hereward! Grabbing a meat hook, he set about them. Their surprise was laughable as the humble potter attacked them ferociously. He was quite outnumbered and, as he had heard enough, he beat a hasty retreat on Swallow, leaving chaos behind him!

So – that was what Hereward had been up to while he was gone!

We were all amazed at his daring as he told us of his

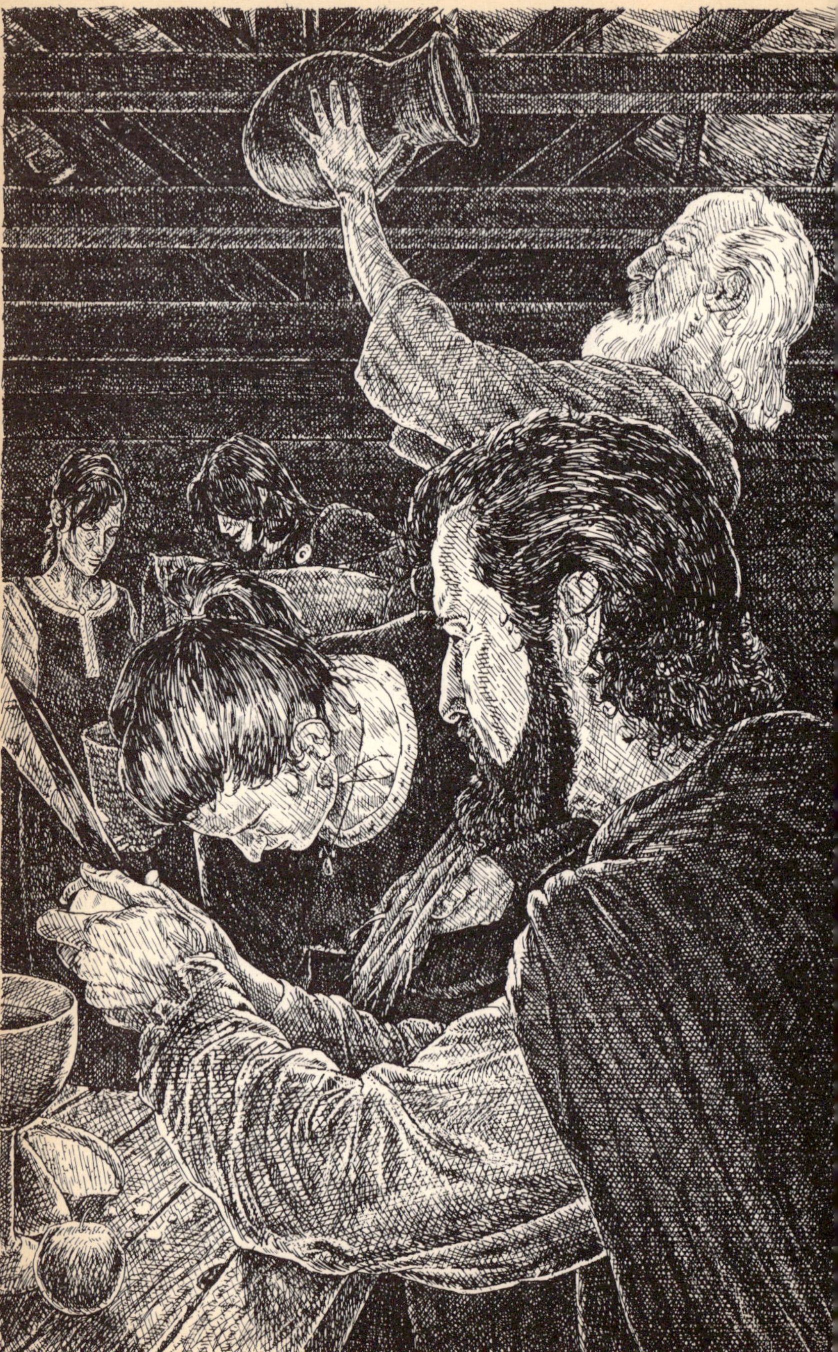

adventures, but Torfrida was quiet, not joining in our laughter. Although she was delighted to see him back, safe and well, she was thinking of the future – of the next attack. William would know the ground this time; he would come well prepared.

Soon, Hereward had us all at work on the edge of the isle, strengthening the rampart and building a fort. Meanwhile, the Normans were busy, too, repairing and rebuilding the causeway. They forced the local people around Willingham to help them and, one day, we noticed Hereward was absent. He had joined the Norman work party and had laboured all day. Then, in the evening, he managed to set fire to the Normans' work and they had to start again!

After this, we made several attempts to ambush the Normans but it was soon obvious that they weren't going to be stopped this time and it wasn't long before a better, stronger causeway was ready.

Hereward assembled us all in the fort. Torfrida was with us, too. We were all grateful for his strength and leadership as we watched the approach of William and Ivo Taillebois, followed by the Norman army and, in their midst, sitting on a tall wooden tower, the evil figure of the old Witch of Brandon. She was chanting wildly and we all felt uneasy – it was a very frightening sight. She called for a thunderstorm and we all waited, but the sky remained a cloudless blue.

The whole army was drawn up, now, on the other side of the water – a terrifying picture. William himself was on the bridge, looking very confident. He waited patiently for the tide to rise and then we heard him give a command. Suddenly, balistas and catapults sent rocks hurtling towards us in the fort. Torfrida seemed to go mad:
'Out!' she screamed. 'Everyone, out! Do not waste your lives!'

She sounded so strange and fierce that we obeyed her and all poured out into the open. Was she going to use her magic powers against the evil Witch of Brandon?

We heard shouts: 'The English are on the run! Strike for Normandy!'

Then we heard the trample of feet and the splash of boats being pushed into the water beside the bridge. A tide of men swept towards us.

Suddenly, Hereward moved into action. He signalled to some of his men. He spoke to them quietly and then, swiftly and silently, he led them away. As they disappeared, I was left with Torfrida and the rest. For one dreadful moment, I thought that Hereward was running away – but I couldn't believe he would do that to us. He must have some plan.

The Normans were so close now; only a few yards of open water separated us. They pushed out boats and canoes and crawled onto them like ants and propelled themselves nearer and nearer, heedless of those who fell into the treacherous water. The whole bridge was swarming with Frenchmen.

Suddenly, Torfrida burst into a frenzied chanting, pointing, with arms outstretched, towards the advancing army. I was terrified. Where was Hereward? Was this the end? Was I going to die at the hands of the French?

Then I saw a puff of smoke, a flame, then another and another, coming from the reeds on the French side. A canoe shot out of the reeds heading for our side. It was Hereward! He was setting fire to the reeds! The army was trapped on the bridge.

The wind began to strengthen as if by magic and clouds of smoke and a wall of flames engulfed the Normans. The noise of crackling filled the air and huge red and yellow flames leapt into the sky. The terrified Normans began to flee in all directions and, as they plunged into the swamp, they were sucked under and down into its black depths.

Hereward appeared, like a ghost, from the smoke. He gave a command and a shower of arrows fell on the Normans at the head of the column. There was total confusion. Those Normans who escaped drowning or arrows were caught by the flames and, to this day, I can hear the dreadful sound of screaming men which echoed across the fens and must have been heard miles away.

I saw no more of the Witch of Brandon and I can only guess what happened to her. In the confusion, she must have fallen from her tower and perhaps one of those ghastly cries was hers as she plunged to her death. I saw William riding for all his might to safety, followed by others who had somehow managed to escape.

Totally exhausted, I sank to my knees. As the clouds of smoke parted, I saw Torfrida rush forward and fling herself into Hereward's arms. He, too, looked quite spent. His sword hung loosely in his hand and black streaks spread across his face. The Normans had been defeated, but at what cost? Would any of us ever be the same again after these dreadful events? Hereward's ruthlessness had been shown today; had he the strength left to continue our fight?

CHAPTER EIGHT

We were never again a united and strong force. Hereward and Torfrida were exhausted; they both knew that William would never give up. And, more importantly, many Saxons were ready to surrender, for they had had enough. We were trapped on the island and when we carried out expeditions for food we were often attacked and men were killed. Gloom and despair settled over our camp. I knew the end was near. Men began to leave, the monks became anxious about William's revenge, and, although Hereward made every effort to make jokes and keep our spirits up, I think he knew he would soon be alone.

The end came suddenly, and unexpectedly. Hereward was away foraging in the fens, when Torfrida came running to me:
'We are betrayed, Martin! All is lost. The monks are going to let the Normans in. Go quickly, find Hereward and warn him.'

'But Torfrida, I cannot leave you. Hereward would never forgive me.'

'Go, Martin! You must go!' screamed Torfrida.

'Hereward will save me.'

She would not be dissuaded, so I left, with all haste, but throughout the journey I was filled with apprehension of Hereward's fury when he heard my news.

I came upon him on his way home. His anger cannot be described. He was like a man possessed by the devil as he rowed back to Ely. The sun was setting as we arrived and we heard the sound of a horse galloping towards us. I could hear my own heart beating and fear filled my whole body.

'Hereward! Oh, thank God I am in time!'

It was Torfrida riding Swallow. She had escaped.

'The French are on the island. We must go,' she gasped.

'No! Onward. We must have revenge!' Hereward shouted.

'Hereward no! You shall not go on. We shall be taken. Hereward, take me away or kill me now!'

Torfrida sobbed and pleaded:
'Let us flee. All is against us. Take me away.'

Hereward turned and looked towards Ely. The sky was black. I felt I could read his thoughts and feel his despair. All his splendid hopes for the future were destroyed by treachery.

Without a word, he turned, defeat written on his face, and we made our way to the boats. Once aboard, we began to row, Swallow swimming behind us as she had done so often. Hereward leaned over the side and I heard a gurgle and a splash. He turned back and blood dripped from his dagger.

'Swallow,' whispered Torfrida.

Hereward's voice was husky:
'Do you think I would ever let a Frenchman say he had ridden Hereward's mare?'

No-one said a word and we rowed away into the night.

We managed to escape and arrived safely in the woods of Northamptonshire. Now we were outlaws, pursued by the Normans. This seemed to restore Hereward and he was again full of determination and anger.

'All is not lost. We shall continue the fight, Martin. We'll burn every town which the French hold. We'll give them no peace!'

So it began. News travelled quickly and many other outlaws joined us. Another band of men took shape; night raids were carried out and excitement grew again. Then we had most unwelcome visitors – Ivo Taillebois, Abbot Turold and a Norman army! But we led them a merry dance! Wearing armour and trying to ride through the low trees in the forest, they had as much trouble as they had had in the fens. All day we kept appearing in the glades and then disappearing; they had no hope of catching us! Hereward was enjoying himself as we lured groups of Normans into ambushes. By dusk they had had enough and turned for home; it was then that Hereward struck. We attacked the rear of the army and Hereward, rushing from the woods, managed to seize Abbot Turold. Revenge at last! We kept him for some time, until we received a ransom, and Hereward thoroughly enjoyed holding him captive.

• • • • •

All that was a long time ago. I am an old man now and I often wonder what happened to Hereward in the end. One day, he simply disappeared; he set out into the forest and never came back. I waited and waited for news, but none came. Eventually, I settled in this part of the country, happy to live a peaceful life yet, at the same time, missing the excitement of those adventurous days. Part of me always hoped that Hereward would reappear. The Normans established control over England and, being only a servant, I escaped capture; I was not important enough to cause them any harm, so they left me in peace.

There have been many rumours about Hereward, but I don't suppose I shall ever know the truth. But I do know that he would have been furious to hear himself called Hereward the *Wake*. This was the surname of a Norman family who owned a manor once stolen from Hereward. He had no connection with them at all.

One story about Hereward made me very sad. I heard that he made his peace with William through a woman call Alftrued, supposedly a girlfriend from his bear-slaying days, who had loved him always. She is supposed to have arranged his reconciliation with the King, in return for marriage. Poor Torfrida was cast aside and sought refuge at Crowland Abbey with Hereward's mother, where she became a nun. There they both ended their days. But it is said that in the end Hereward went back to Bourne and, at the time of his death, begged to be buried with Torfrida, his one true love.

However, I prefer to believe yet another version of the story; this seems a fitting end for the hero of my youth. After his reconciliation with William, I heard that Hereward was ordered to join Norman forces on an expedition to quell a rebellion on the borders of Normandy. But he never left because a group of Norman knights, who could never forgive Hereward, heard of his surrender to the King and set upon him. Hereward was unprepared and, taken completely unawares, he only had time to grab his shield and sword and a javelin, which he hurled through the air, straight into the heart of one knight. Then, the rest of the knights attacked, surrounding him and wounding him.

Hereward fought like a savage. He killed four with his sword and, when this broke, he took his shield in both hands and killed two more. But he was overpowered at last. Four men came at his back and ran him through with lances. He sank down onto his knees and, with the last of his ebbing strength hurled his shield so hard that it broke a knight's neck.

So, Hereward died.

A Norman knight bent down and cut off Hereward's head. As he did so, he said:
'Had there been three more like him, we would never have conquered England.'

Yes, this is surely how Hereward would have wanted to die. A noble man, brave, hot-headed and true to his country. My hero, and a hero who will long be remembered in England.

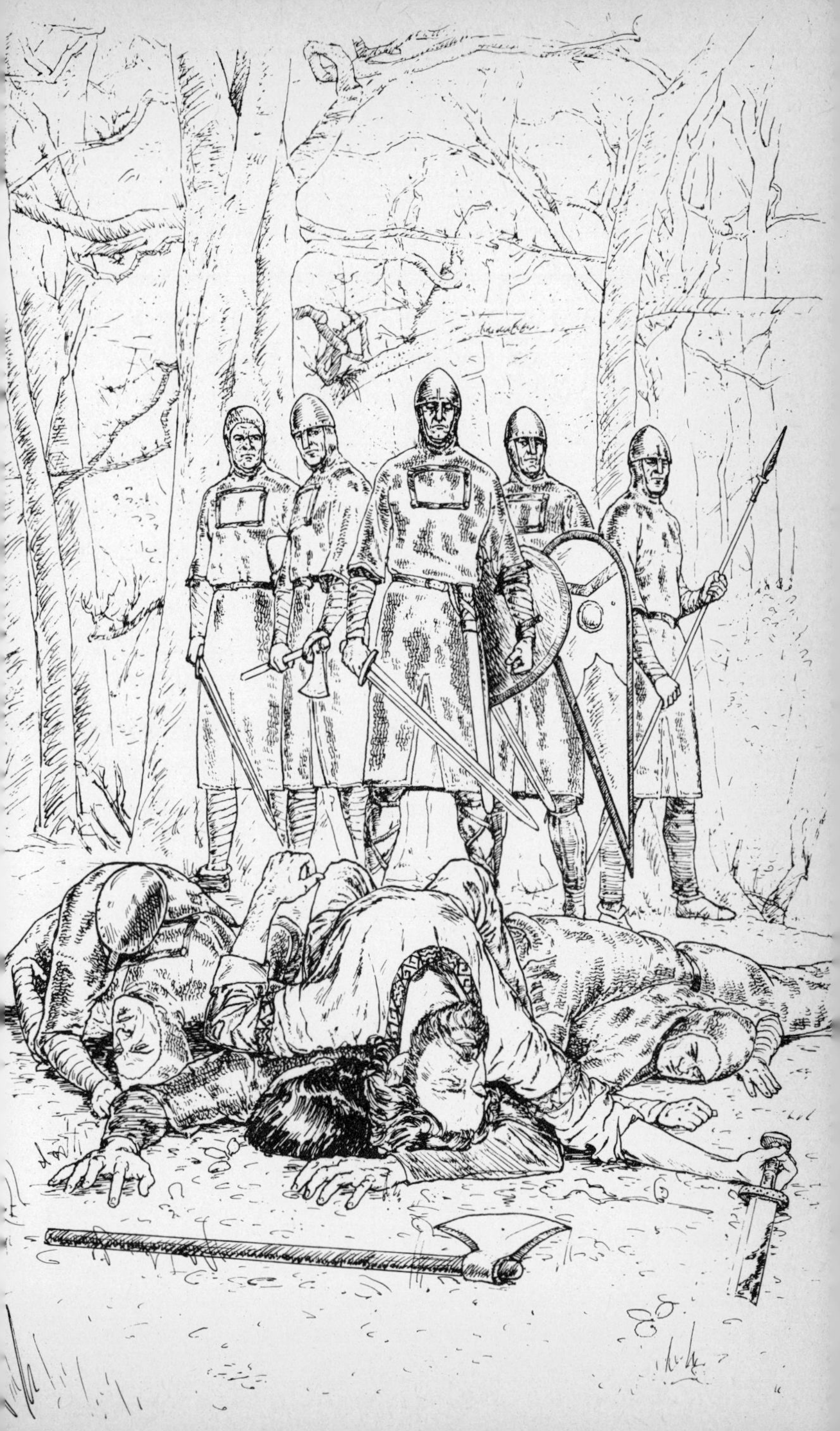

PLACES TO VISIT

Ely Cathedral

Peterborough and the ruins of Crowland Abbey

Castle Mound (Castle Hill, Cambridge)

Wicken Fen

Mountfitchet Castle and
Norman Village, Stansted

Printed in Great Britain
by Amazon

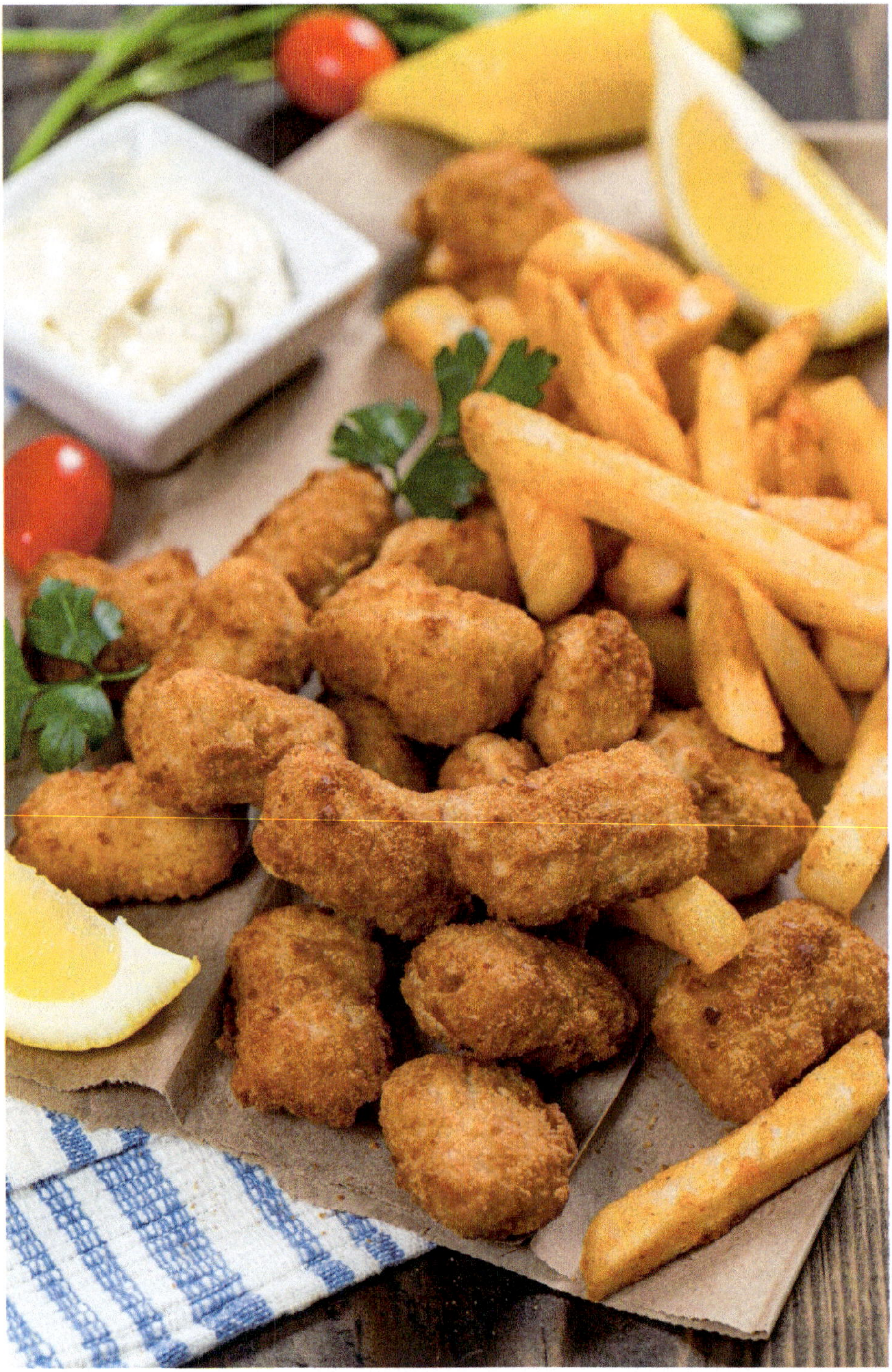

CREDITS

Icon made by [Pixel perfect](#) from [www.flaticon.com](#)

Tuna Patties	51
Turkey And Mushroom Burgers	30

V

Vegetable Frittata	21

INDEX

A
Apple Chips	67
Aubergine Sticks	62

B
Bacon Muffins	19
Baked Crunchy Cod	54
Beef Fried Rice	35
Beef Kebobs	38
Beef Wellington	44
Beef Wellington	45
British Victoria Sponge	65
Broccoli with Oil	57
Brussels Sprouts	63

C
Cheese Omelette	23
Cheesy Beef Enchiladas	42
Chicken Breast	32
Chicken Nuggets	28
Chicken Parmesan	34
Chicken Strips	29
Chicken Tenders	26
Chicken Wings with Honey and Sesame	25
Chocolate Chip Cookies	20
Coconut Prawns	46
Courgette Sticks	58
Crab Cakes	47
Creamy Chocolate Eclairs	66

E
Egg & Ham Cups	16

F
Fish Tacos	49
French Toast Sticks	24
Fried Bacon	17
Fried Chips	56
Fried Cod	52
Fried Pickles	61
Fruit Crumble	70

G
Garlic Cauliflower	55
Garlic Herb Turkey Breast	31
Green Beans	64

H
Herbed Steak	36

L
Lamb Steaks	41
Lemon Biscuits	68

M
Mini Apple Pie	71
Mozzarella Sticks	59
Mozzarella-Stuffed Meatballs	37
Mustard Glazed Pork	40

P
Patatas Bravas	18
Peppery Lemon Shrimp	50
Pork Chops	39

R
Roast Potatoes	60
Rotisserie Chicken	27

S
Sausage Sandwiches	22
Shortbread Chocolate Balls	72
Simple Hamburgers	43
Soft Chocolate Brownies	69
Spicy Chicken Thighs	33
Sriracha With Salmon	53
Strawberry Cupcakes	73
Sweet Potato Hash	15

T
Tilapia Fillets	48

STRAWBERRY CUPCAKES

15 minutes | 8 minutes | 10

INGREDIENTS

- 100 g Butter
- 100 g Caster Sugar
- 2 Medium Eggs
- 100 g Self Raising Flour
- ½ tsp. Vanilla Essence
- 50 g Butter
- 100 g Icing Sugar
- ½ tsp. Pink Food Colouring
- 1 tbsp. Whipped Cream
- 40 g Fresh Strawberries (blended)

DIRECTIONS

1. Preheat the Air Fryer to 170°C.
2. Meanwhile, cream the sugar and butter using a large mixing bowl. Do this until your mixture is light and fluffy.
3. Add the vanilla essence and beat in the eggs one at a time. After adding each egg add a little of the flour. Gently fold in the reamining flour.
4. Add them to little bun cases so that they are 80% full.
5. Place them in the Air Fryer and then cook for 8 minutes on 170°C.
6. Meanwhile make the topping: Cream the butter and gradually add the icing sugar until you have a creamy mixture. Add the food colouring, whipped cream and blended strawberries and mix well.
7. Once the cupcakes are cooked, using a piping bag add your topping to them doing circular motions so that you have that lovely cupcake look.
8. Serve!

Nutrition: Calories: 231; Fat: 13 g; Protein: 2.5 g; Carbs: 26 g; Fiber: 1 g; Sugar: 19 g

SHORTBREAD CHOCOLATE BALLS

4 minutes | 13 minutes | 9

INGREDIENTS

- 175 g Butter
- 75 g Caster Sugar
- 250 g Plain Flour
- 1 tsp. Vanilla Essence
- 9 Chocolate chunks
- 2 tbsp. Cocoa

DIRECTIONS

1. Preheat your Air Fryer to 180°C.
2. Take a bowl and mix your sugar, flour, and cocoa.
3. Rub in the butter, knead well until you see a smooth dough.
4. Now divide into balls, place a chunk of chocolate into the centre of each one, make sure none of the chocolate chunk is showing.
5. Place your chocolate shortbread balls onto a baking sheet in your Air Fryer. Cook them at 180°C for 8 minutes and then a further 5 minutes on 160°C so that you can make sure they are cooked in the middle.
6. Serve!

Nutrition: Calories: 297; Fat: 18 g; Protein: 4 g; Carbs: 31 g; Fiber: 3.5 g; Sugar: 10 g

MINI APPLE PIE

5 minutes | 18 minutes | 9

INGREDIENTS

- 75 g Plain Flour
- 33 g Butter
- 15 g Caster Sugar
- Water
- 2 Medium Red Apples
- Pinch Cinnamon
- Pinch Caster Sugar

DIRECTIONS

1. Preheat your Air Fryer to 180°C.
2. Start by making your pastry – place the plain flour and butter in a mixing bowl and rub the fat into the flour. Add the sugar and mix well. Add the water until the ingredients are moist enough to combine into a nice dough. Knead the dough well until it has a smooth texture.
3. Cover your pastry tins with butter to stop it sticking and then roll out the pastry and fill your pastry tins.
4. Peel, dice your apples, place in the tins. Sprinkle them with sugar and cinnamon.
5. Add an extra pastry layer to the top and make some fork markings so that they can breathe.
6. Cook in the Air Fryer for 18 minutes.

Nutrition: Calories: 85; Fat: 3 g; Protein: 1 g; Carbs: 13.5 g; Fiber: 1.5 g; Sugar: 6.5 g

FRUIT CRUMBLE

15 minutes | 15 minutes | 6

INGREDIENTS

- 75 g Plain Flour
- 33 g Butter
- 30 g Caster Sugar
- 1 Medium Red Apple70
- 4 Medium Plums
- 50 g Frozen Berries
- 1 tsp. Cinnamon

DIRECTIONS

1. Preheat your Air Fryer to 180°C.
2. Take a suitable dish that will fit in your Air Fryer, then add the fruit. Peel and dice everything, check it is all of a similar size.
3. Place plain flour in a mixing bowl along with sugar and mix in the butter. Rub fat into the flour until your mixture resembles breadcrumbs.
4. Arrange your crumble mixture over the fruit and place into the Air Fryer.
5. Cook 15 minutes, 180°C.
6. Serve!

Nutrition: Calories: 141; Fat: 4.5 g; Protein: 1.6 g; Carbs: 24 g; Fiber: 2.5 g; Sugar: 13 g

SOFT CHOCOLATE BROWNIES

20 minutes | 18 minutes | 10

INGREDIENTS

- 125 g Caster Sugar
- 2 tbsp. Water
- 142 ml Milk
- 125 g Butter
- 50 g Chocolate
- 175 g Brown Sugar
- 2 Medium Eggs (beaten)
- 100 g Self Raising Flour
- 2 tsp. Vanilla Essence

DIRECTIONS

1. Preheat your Air Fryer to 180°C.
2. Prepare the chocolate brownies: Melt 100 g of butter and the chocolate in a bowl above a pan, over medium heat. Stir in the brown sugar, now add the eggs and then add the vanilla essence. Add the self raising flour and mix well.
3. Pour the mixture into a greased dish that is of an appropriate size for your Air Fryer.
4. Cook into the Air Fryer for 15 minutes, 180°C.
5. While the brownies are cooking it is time to make the caramel sauce – Mix the caster sugar and the water in a pan on a medium heat until the sugar is melted. Then turn it up and cook for a further three minutes until it has turned a light brown colour. Take off the heat and then after 2 minutes add your butter and keep stirring until it is all melted. Then slowly add the milk.
6. Set the caramel sauce to one side for it to cool.
7. When the brownies are ready chop them into squares and place them on a plate with some sliced banana and cover with some caramel sauce.
8. Serve!

Nutrition: Calories: 249; Fat: 13 g; Protein: 3.5 g; Carbs: 30 g; Fiber: 1.5 g; Sugar: 21.5 g

LEMON BISCUITS

5 minutes   5 minutes   9

INGREDIENTS

- 100 g Butter
- 100 g Caster Sugar
- 225 g Self Raising Flour
- 1 Small Lemon (rind and juice)
- 1 Small Egg
- 1 tsp. Vanilla Essence

DIRECTIONS

1. Preheat the Air Fryer to 180°C.
2. Mix flour and sugar in a bowl. Add the butter and rub it in until your mix resembles breadcrumbs. Shake your bowl regularly so that the fat bits come to the top and so that you know what you have left to rub in.
3. Add the lemon rind and juice along with the egg.
4. Combine and knead until you have lovely soft dough.
5. Roll out and cut into medium sized biscuits.
6. Place the biscuits into the Air Fryer on a baking sheet and cook for five minutes at 180°C.
7. Place on a cooling tray and sprinkle with icing sugar

Nutrition: Calories: 205; Fat: 10 g; Protein: 3.5 g; Carbs: 26 g; Fiber: 2.5 g; Sugar: 10 g

APPLE CHIPS

2 minutes   10 minutes   1

INGREDIENTS
- 6 Large Red Apples
- 1 tsp. Olive Oil
- 1 Pinch Cinnamon

DIRECTIONS
1. Slide up your apple into nice bite sized chunks.
2. Place them in the Air Fryer and drizzle with a teaspoon of olive oil.
3. Cook on a 180°C for 10 minutes or until nice and crisp.
4. Toss them in cinnamon in a large bowl.
5. Serve!

Nutrition: Calories: 666; Fat: 6 g; Protein: 3 g; Carbs: 165 g; Fiber: 16 g; Sugar: 130 g

CREAMY CHOCOLATE ECLAIRS

15 minutes   25 minutes   9

INGREDIENTS

Éclair Dough:
- 50 g Butter
- 100 g Plain Flour
- 3 Medium Eggs
- 150 ml Water

Cream Filling:
- 1 tsp. Vanilla Essence
- 1 tsp. Icing Sugar
- 150 ml Whipped Cream

Chocolate Topping:
- 50 g Milk 181(chopped into chunks)
- 1 tbsp. Whipped Cream
- 25 g Butter

DIRECTIONS

1. Preheat the Air Fryer to 180°C.
2. While it is heating up, place the fat in the water, melt over medium heat, using a large pan, then bring to the boil.
3. Now remove it from the heat and stir in the flour.
4. Place the pan again to the heat and stir into it forms a medium ball in the middle of the pan.
5. Transfer the dough to a cold plate so that it can cool. Once it is cool beat in the eggs until you have a smooth mixture.
6. Then make into éclair shapes and place in the Air Fryer. Cook for 10 minutes on 180°C and a further 8 minutes on 160°C.
7. While the dough is cooking make your cream filling: Mix with a whisk the whipped cream, vanilla essence and icing sugar until nice and thick.
8. Leave the eclairs to cool and while they are cooling make your chocolate topping – Place the milk chocolate, whipped cream and butter into a glass bowl. Place it over a pan of hot water and mix well until you have melted chocolate.
9. Cover the tops of the eclairs with melted chocolate and then serve!

Nutrition: Calories: 181; Fat: 13 g; Protein: 4 g; Carbs: 27.5 g; Fiber: 1.5 g; Sugar: 3 g

CHAPTER 6: DESSERT RECIPES

BRITISH VICTORIA SPONGE

15 minutes | 28 minutes | 8

INGREDIENTS

For the Victoria Sponge:
- 100 g Plain Flour
- 100 g Butter
- 100 g Caster Sugar
- 2 Medium Eggs

For the Cake Filling:
- 2 tbsp. Strawberry Jam
- 50 g Butter
- 100 g Icing Sugar
- 1 tbsp. Whipped Cream

DIRECTIONS

1. Preheat the Air Fryer to 180°C.
2. Grease a baking dish.
3. Cream the sugar and the butter until light and fluffy.
4. Now beat in the eggs, add a little flour with each.
5. Now gently fold in the flour.
6. Arrange your mixture into the tin and cook for 15 minutes, 180°C, then 10 minutes, 170°C.
7. Now leave it to cool and once it is cooled slice into two equal slices of sponge.
8. Now make the filling: Cream the butter, until you have a thick creamy mixture gradually add icing sugar and whipped cream.
9. Arrange a layer of strawberry jam, then a layer of cake filling, then add your other sponge on top.
10. Serve!

Nutrition: Calories: 243; Fat: 16.5 g; Protein: 3 g; Carbs: 21 g; Fiber: 1 g; Sugar: 12 g

GREEN BEANS

2 minutes | 7 minutes | 2

INGREDIENTS

- 1 tsp. of lemon juice
- 1/2 tsp. of Garlic Powder
- 320 g of Fresh Green Beans
- 1 tsp. of Olive oil
- 1/2 tsp. of Salt
- 1/2 tsp. of Ground Pepper
- 1/2 tsp. of Italian Seasoning

Optional Garnish:

- Lemon Wedge
- Herbs- Parsley Thyme
- Chilli Flakes

DIRECTIONS

1. Trim the beans.
2. Prepare a seasoning mixture with all the ingredients except the beans.
3. Now pour the mixture on the beans, toss to coat well.
4. Preheat your Air Fryer at 200°C, 2 minutes.
5. Arrange the beans inside.
6. Air fry 7-8 minutes, 200°C.
7. Serve with optional garnish.

Nutrition: Calories: 50.5; Fat: 0.5 g; Protein: 2.5 g; Carbs: 10 g; Fiber: 4 g; Sugar: 4.5 g

BRUSSELS SPROUTS

14 minutes | 20 minutes | 4

INGREDIENTS

- 450 g Brussels sprouts, trimmed and cut in half
- 1 tbsp. extra-virgin olive oil
- Salt
- Freshly ground black pepper
- Pinch crushed chilli flakes
- Juice of 1/2 lemon
- 1 tbsp. honey
- 1 tbsp. red wine vinegar
- 2 tsp. Dijon mustard
- 1 clove garlic, crushed

DIRECTIONS

1. Take a medium bowl, add brussels sprouts, oil and season with salt, pepper, and chilli flakes. Toss around to coat brussels sprouts well.
2. Arrange the brussels sprouts into the Air Fryer basket, working in batches as needed, and cook at 190°C, 18 minutes, stopping and tossing brussels in basket halfway through.
3. Meanwhile make the dressing: Take a small bowl, whisk together mustard, lemon juice, honey, vinegar, and garlic. Add salt and pepper.
4. Place the Brussels sprouts into a medium bowl, pour the dressing over and toss.

Nutrition: Calories: 94; Fat: 3.5 g; Protein: 4 g; Carbs: 14 g; Fiber: 4 g; Sugar: 6.5 g

AUBERGINE STICKS

9 minutes | 15 minutes | 4

INGREDIENTS

- 1 medium aubergine
- 1 tbsp. extra-virgin olive oil
- 1 tsp. dried oregano
- 1/2 tsp. garlic powder
- Salt
- Freshly ground black pepper
- Pinch chilli flakes

DIRECTIONS

1. Take the aubergine and cut the ends off, then cut it in half (lengthwise). Now cut each half into strips about 2.5 cm thick and 7 cm long. Take a medium bowl, add oil, aubergine, and seasonings, toss to coat.
2. Arrange a single layer into the Air Fryer basket. Cook 190°C 14 minutes, until golden, shake the basket once about halfway through.

Nutrition: Calories: 58; Fat: 3.5 g; Protein: 1 g; Carbs: 6.5 g; Fiber: 3 g; Sugar: 4 g

FRIED PICKLES

10 minutes   10 minutes   3

INGREDIENTS

- 300 g dill pickle slices
- 1 egg, whisked with 1 tbsp. water
- 50 g bread crumbs
- 25 g freshly grated Parmesan
- 1 tsp. dried oregano
- 1 tsp. garlic powder
- Ranch, for dipping

DIRECTIONS

1. Using paper towels, pat pickle chips dry. In a medium bowl, stir together bread crumbs, Parmesan, oregano, and garlic powder.
2. Dredge pickle chips first in egg and then in the bread crumb mixture. Arrange a single layer into the Air Fryer basket. Cook at 200°C for 10 minutes.
3. Serve warm with ranch.

Nutrition: Calories: 115; Fat: 3.5 g; Protein: 6 g; Carbs: 11 g; Fiber: 1 g; Sugar: 2 g

ROAST POTATOES

< 30 minutes | 30-60 minutes | 2

INGREDIENTS

- 2 large **floury potatoes** (approximately 450g)
- **salt**, to taste
- 1 tbsp. **olive oil**

DIRECTIONS

1. Peel, quarter your potatoes, then boil them in a saucepan of salted water for 15 minutes (place them when the water is already boiling).
2. Now drain the potatoes, leave them to steam dry for a minute or two.
3. Toss with olive oil and a good amount of salt.
4. Air fry 30 minutes, 200°C, toss every 10 minutes.
5. Serve.

Nutrition: Calories: 232.5; Fat: 7 g; Protein: 4.5 g; Carbs: 39 g; Fiber: 4.5 g; Sugar: 1.5 g

MOZZARELLA STICKS

30-60 minutes | 10-30 minutes | 3-4

INGREDIENTS

- 400 g block mozzarella cucina
- 2 tbsp. plain flour
- 1 tsp. garlic granules
- 1 large free-range egg
- 40g panko 369
- olive oil cooking spray
- salt and freshly ground black pepper

DIRECTIONS

1. Cut the mozzarella into strips, roughly 1.5 cm wide, pat dry using some kitchen paper.
2. In a shallow dish, combine flour and garlic granules. Take another dish, beat the egg and add a good amount of salt and pepper. Now spread the breadcrumbs in a third dish.
3. Roll your mozzarella strips into the flour, then into the egg, then into the flour and into the egg again, to create double coating. Check that each piece is totally covered in the flour each time. Coat well in the panko breadcrumbs.
4. Freeze 30 minutes or more, until solid.
5. Spray the bottom of your Air Fryer basket with olive oil spray, place a single layer of mozzarella sticks at the bottom. Now spray the top of the mozzarella sticks with oil, air fry 10 minutes, 200°C. Now repeat until all your mozzarella sticks are cooked, keeping each batch warm, then serve immediately.

Nutrition: Calories: 369; Fat: 23.5 g; Protein: 25 g; Carbs: 12 g; Fiber: 1 g; Sugar: 2 g

COURGETTE STICKS

10 minutes | 20 minutes | 4

INGREDIENTS

- 2 medium courgette, sliced into 1/2cm rounds
- 2 large eggs
- 90 g panko bread crumbs
- 50 g cornmeal
- 35 g freshly grated 182
- 1 tsp. dried oregano
- 1/4 tsp. garlic powder
- Pinch chilli flakes
- Salt
- Freshly ground black pepper
- Marinara, for serving

DIRECTIONS

1. Arrange the courgette on a platter lined with paper towels and pat dry.
2. Arrange the beaten eggs in a shallow bowl. Take another shallow bowl, mix cornmeal, panko, oregano, Parmesan, garlic powder, and a large pinch of chilli flakes. Add salt and pepper.
3. One at a time, dip the courgette rounds into the egg, then into the panko mixture, press to coat.
4. Arrange the courgette in an even layer, cook at 200°C 18 minutes, flip halfway through.
5. Serve warm with marinara.

Nutrition: Calories: 182; Fat: 5 g; Protein: 6.6 g; Carbs: 22 g; Fiber: 1 g; Sugar: 2 g

BROCCOLI WITH OIL

5 minutes   10 minutes   4

INGREDIENTS

- 1 medium head broccoli, cut into florets
- 1 tbsp. extra-virgin olive oil
- 1 clove garlic, crushed
- Salt
- Freshly ground black pepper
- Pinch chilli flakes

DIRECTIONS

1. Take a large bowl, toss broccoli with garlic and oil. Season with salt, pepper, chilli flakes.
2. Arrange the broccoli in a single layer inside the basket. Cook 10 minutes 180°C, until tender and crisp. Repeat with the remaining part.

Nutrition: Calories: 81; Fat: 4 g; Protein: 4 g; Carbs: 10 g; Fiber: 4 g; Sugar: 3 g

FRIED CHIPS

5 minutes   20 minutes   4

INGREDIENTS

- Salt
- 1 kg of potatoes, peeled, cut into 1cm batons
- Oil spray (vegetable or sunflower works best)
- Other optional seasoning
- Your favourite dip

DIRECTIONS

1. Preheat to 180°C. Rinse the chips in cold water then pat them dry.
2. Place the chips into the Air Fryer basket and spray with oil. Sprinkle them with salt and any other seasoning you want, then shake the basket.
3. Air fry for 20 minutes, shake the chips halfway through to ensure even cooking. After it finishes, if the chips are not well cooked, place them back inside for 5 minutes more and continue to do so until they are good to go.
4. Serve with your favourite dip.

Nutrition: Calories: 192.5; Fat: 0 g; Protein: 5 g; Carbs: 43.5 g; Fiber: 5 g; Sugar: 2 g

CHAPTER 5: SIDE DISH RECIPES

GARLIC CAULIFLOWER

10 minutes   15 minutes   2-3

INGREDIENTS

- 2 tbsp. ghee or butter, melted
- Freshly ground black pepper
- 1/2 tsp. garlic powder
- 1/4 tsp. turmeric
- Salt
- 1 small head of 114.5cut into small florets

DIRECTIONS

1. Take a small bowl and whisk turmeric, ghee, garlic powder. Place cauliflower in a large bowl, pour over the ghee mixture, toss to coat until all the florets are yellow. Add a good amount of salt and pepper.
2. Preheat your Air Fryer to 190°C, 3 minutes. Arrange the cauliflower in a single layer into the basket and cook, toss halfway through, until golden brown, 10-12 minutes.

Nutrition: Calories: 114.5; Fat: 11.5 g; Protein: 1 g; Carbs: 2.5 g; Fiber: 1 g; Sugar: 1 g

BAKED CRUNCHY COD

10 minutes | 15 minutes | 2

INGREDIENTS

- 2 pieces of cod cut into smaller portions (around five)
- 4 tbsp. of panko breadcrumbs
- 1 egg
- 1 egg white
- ½ tsp. onion powder
- ½ tsp. garlic salt
- A pinch of pepper
- ½ tsp. mixed herbs

DIRECTIONS

1. Heat Air Fryer to 220°C
2. Take a small bowl and mix the egg and then add the egg white and combine once more
3. Cover the top of the fish with the herb mixture
4. Dip each piece of fish into the egg and then cover in the panko breadcrumbs
5. Line Air Fryer basket with tin foil
6. Place the fish in Air Fryer and cook for about 15 minutes

Nutrition: Calories: 291; Fat: 4 g; Protein: 45 g; Carbs: 12 g; Fiber: 0.5 g; Sugar: 1 g

SRIRACHA WITH SALMON

35 minutes　　　　15 minutes　　　　2

INGREDIENTS

- 3 tbsp. sriracha
- 4 tbsp. honey
- 1 tbsp. soy sauce
- 500 g salmon fillets

DIRECTIONS

1. Take a medium bowl and add the honey, soy sauce and sriracha, combining well
2. Place the salmon into the sauce skin, with the skin facing upwards
3. Allow to marinade for 30 minutes
4. Spray the basket with some cooking spray.
5. Heat the Air Fryer to 200°C
6. Place the salmon into the Air Fryer skin side down and cook for 12 minutes
7. Serve!

Nutrition: Calories: 505; Fat: 15 g; Protein: 50 g; Carbs: 38.5 g; Fiber: 0.5 g; Sugar: 37.5 g

FRIED COD

15 minutes   15 minutes   3

INGREDIENTS

- 1 (450g) cod, cut into 4 strips
- Salt
- Freshly ground black pepper
- 65 g plain flour
- 1 large egg, beaten
- 200 g panko bread crumbs
- 1 tsp. Old Bay seasoning
- Lemon wedges, for serving
- Tartar sauce, for serving

DIRECTIONS

1. Pat the fish dry and add salt and pepper on both sides.
2. Arrange egg, flour, and panko in three shallow bowls. Add Old Bay to panko and toss. Coat fish into the flour, then into the egg, and finally into panko, press to coat, one at a time.
3. Arrange the fish into the Air Fryer basket, cook 10-12 minutes, 200°C, or until fish is golden and flakes easily with a fork, gently flip halfway through.
4. Serve with lemon wedges and tartar sauce.

Nutrition: Calories: 397; Fat: 4.5 g; Protein: 37 g; Carbs: 48 g; Fiber: 3.5 g; Sugar: 3.5 g

TUNA PATTIES

15 minutes | 10 minutes | 10

INGREDIENTS

- 425 g canned albacore tuna, drained or 454g fresh tuna, diced
- 2-3 large eggs
- zest of 1 medium lemon
- 1 tbsp. lemon juice
- 1/4 tsp of Kosher salt, or to taste
- 55 g of bread crumbs
- 1/2 tsp dried herbs (oregano, dill, basil, thyme or any combo)
- fresh cracked black pepper
- 3 tbsp grated parmesan cheese
- 1 stalk celery, finely chopped
- Optional: tarter sauce, ranch, mayo, lemon slices
- 3 tbsp minced onion
- 1/2 tsp garlic powder

DIRECTIONS

1. Take a medium bowl, mix the lemon zest, eggs, lemon juice, bread crumbs, celery, parmesan cheese, onion, dried herbs, garlic powder, salt, pepper. Now stir well. Gently fold in the tuna.
2. Take your Air Fryer perforated baking paper, lay it inside the base of the Air Fryer. Now lightly spray the paper. if not you don't have it spray at the base of the Air Fryer basket to make sure they do not stick.
3. Try to keep all patties same size and thickness. Scoop 1/4 cup of the mixture, shape into patties about 8 cm wide x 1.3 cm thick and lay them inside the basket. Makes about 10 patties.
4. If patties are too soft, chill them for 1 hour or until firm. Brush the top of the patties with oil. Air Fry 185°C, 10 minutes, flip halfway through. After you flip the patties, spray the tops again.
5. Serve with your sauce and lemon slices.

Nutrition: Calories: 102.2; Fat: 3.9 g; Protein: 12.5 g; Carbs: 2.7 g; Fiber: 0 g; Sugar: 0 g

PEPPERY LEMON SHRIMP

10 minutes | 10 minutes | 2

INGREDIENTS

- 1 tbsp. olive oil
- 350g prepared 208, uncooked
- Juice of 1 lemon
- 1 tsp. pepper
- ¼ tsp. paprika
- ¼ tsp. garlic powder
- 1 lemon, sliced

DIRECTIONS

1. Preheat the fryer to 200°C
2. Take a medium size mixing bowl, mix the pepper, lemon juice, garlic powder, paprika and the olive oil together
3. Add the shrimp to the bowl and make sure they're well coated
4. Arrange the shrimp into the basket of the fryer
5. Cook for between 6-8 minutes, until firm and pink
6. Serve!

Nutrition: Calories: 208; Fat: 7 g; Protein: 35 g; Carbs: 0 g; Fiber: 0 g; Sugar: 0 g

FISH TACOS

14 minutes   10 minutes   4

INGREDIENTS

- 500g mahi fish, fresh
- 8 small tortillas
- 2 tsp. Cajun seasoning
- 4 tbsp. sour cream
- 2 tbsp. mayo
- ¼ tbsp. cayenne
- 2 tbsp. pepper sauce
- A little salt and pepper
- 1 tbsp. sriracha sauce
- 2 tbsp. lime juice

DIRECTIONS

1. Cut the fish into slices and season with salt
2. Mix the cayenne pepper and black pepper with the Cajun seasoning. Sprinkle onto fish
3. Brush pepper sauce on both sides of the fish
4. Set Air Fryer to 180°C and cook for 10 mins
5. Take a medium bowl and combine the mayonnaise, sour cream, lime juice, sriracha and cayenne pepper
6. Assemble tacos the tacos and serve!

Nutrition: Calories: 447; Fat: 13 g; Protein: 31 g; Carbs: 48 g; Fiber: 3 g; Sugar: 3.5 g

TILAPIA FILLETS

10 minutes | 10 minutes | 2

INGREDIENTS

- 50g almond flour
- 2 fillets of tilapia fish
- 2 tbsp. melted butter
- 1 tsp. black pepper
- ½ tsp. salt
- 4 tbsp. mayonnaise
- A handful of almonds, sliced thinly

DIRECTIONS

1. Take a mixing bowl and add the butter, almond flour, pepper and salt, combining well
2. Take the fish and spread the mayonnaise on both sides
3. Cover the fillets in the almond flour mix
4. Spread one side of the fish with the sliced almonds
5. Spray your Air Fryer with a little amount of cooking spray.
6. Add the fish into the Air Fryer and cook at 160°C for 10 minutes

Nutrition: Calories: 500; Fat: 30.5 g; Protein: 33 g; Carbs: 25 g; Fiber: 7 g; Sugar: 1.5 g

CRAB CAKES

20 minutes | 15 minutes | 4

INGREDIENTS

For The Crab Cakes:
- Cooking spray
- Hot sauce, for serving
- Lemon wedges, for serving
- 60 g of mayonnaise
- 1 egg
- 2 tsp. of cajun seasoning
- 1 tsp. of lemon zest
- 1/2 tsp. of salt
- 450 g of jumbo lump crab meat
- 120 g of Cracker crumbs (from about 20 crackers)
- 2 tbsp. of chives, finely chopped
- 2 tsp. of Dijon mustard

For The Tartar Sauce:
- 1/4 tsp. of Dijon mustard
- 1 tsp. of fresh dill, finely chopped
- 60 g of mayonnaise
- 80 g dill pickle, finely chopped
- 2 tsp. of capers, finely chopped
- 1 tsp. of fresh lemon juice
- 1 tbsp. of shallot, finely chopped

DIRECTIONS

1. Take a large bowl, whisk together egg, mayo, chives, Dijon mustard, lemon zest, cajun seasoning, and salt. Fold in crab meat and cracker crumbs.
2. Divide your mixture to form 8 patties.
3. Heat your Air Fryer to 190°C, spray the basket and the tops of your cakes with some cooking spray. Arrange the cakes into the basket in a single layer. Cook until crisp and deep golden brown, 12-14 minutes, flip halfway through.
4. Take a bowl and mix all of the tartar sauce ingredients.
5. Serve the cakes warm with lemon wedges, hot sauce and tartar sauce.

Nutrition: Calories: 265; Fat: 8 g; Protein: 24.5 g; Carbs: 21 g; Fiber: 1 g; Sugar: 0 g

COCONUT PRAWNS

15 minutes | 15 minutes | 4

INGREDIENTS

For The Prawns:
- 450 g of large prawns, peeled, deveined, tails on
- Freshly ground black pepper
- 65 g of plain flour
- Salt
- 35 g of shredded sweetened coconut
- 2 large eggs, beaten
- 100 g of panko bread crumbs

For The Dipping Sauce:
- 1 tbsp. of Sriracha
- 1 tbsp. of Thai sweet chilli sauce
- 120 g of mayonnaise

DIRECTIONS

1. Take a shallow bowl, add salt and pepper to flour. Take another shallow bowl, mix bread crumbs and coconut. Arrange the eggs in a third shallow bowl.
2. Dip prawns in flour, then eggs, then coconut mixture, one at a time.
3. Arrange your prawns into the Air Fryer basket, heat to 200°C. Bake until the prawns are well golden and cooked through, 10-12 minutes.
4. Take a small bowl, mix Siracha, mayonnaise, chilli sauce.
5. Serve with dipping sauce.

Nutrition: Calories: 283; Fat: 6.5 g; Protein: 29 g; Carbs: 25 g; Fiber: 3 g; Sugar: 2 g

CHAPTER 4: FISH AND SEAFOOD RECIPES

BEEF WELLINGTON

5 minutes | 20-25 minutes | 4

INGREDIENTS

- 4 salmon filets
- 3 lemons
- 8 sprigs rosemary
- 1 Tablespoon olive oil
- Salt

DIRECTIONS

1. Slice the lemons into thin slices.
2. Place several lemon slices on the bottom of the Air Fryer basket.
3. Now lay 4 rosemary sprigs on the lemons.
4. Arrange one salmon filet on top of each sprig of rosemary. Sprinkle some salt on the salmon.
5. Top each salmon filet with another sprig of rosemary. Cover with more lemon slices.
6. Drizzle with the olive oil on top.
7. Put the fry basket in the fryer. Set the temperature to 135°C. Set the timer for 20 minutes.
8. Take a fork and check the salmon, If it flakes easily, it's ready. If not, it needs 5 minutes more.
9. Serve the salmon with roasted lemon slices and rosemary.

Nutrition: Calories: 242; Fat: 12 g; Protein: 29 g; Carbs: 0 g; Fiber: 0 g; Sugar: 0 g

BEEF WELLINGTON

15 minutes   35 minutes   8

INGREDIENTS

- 1kg beef fillet (one large piece)
- Chicken pate
- 2 sheets of shortcrust pastry
- 1 egg, beaten
- Salt
- Pepper

DIRECTIONS

1. Season the beef with salt, pepper and wrap tightly in cling film
2. Place the beef in the refrigerator for at least one hour
3. Roll out the pastry and brush the edges with the beaten egg
4. Spread the pate over the pastry, making sure it is distributed equally
5. Take now the beef out of the refrigerator and remove the cling film
6. Place the beef in the middle of your pastry
7. Wrap your pastry around the meat and seal the edges with a fork
8. Place in the Air Fryer and cook at 160°C for 35 minutes

Nutrition: Calories: 509; Fat: 28 g; Protein: 34 g; Carbs: 28 g; Fiber: 1 g; Sugar: 0.5 g

SIMPLE HAMBURGERS

5 minutes 15 minutes 4

INGREDIENTS

- 500 g minced beef
- Salt
- Pepper

DIRECTIONS

1. Preheat Air Fryer to 200°C.
2. Divide minced beef into 4 equal portions and form them into burgers with your hands.
3. Season with salt, pepper, to your taste.
4. Air fry for 10 minutes.
5. Flip your burgers over, cook for a further 3 minutes.

Nutrition: Calories: 247.5; Fat: 15 g; Protein: 24 g; Carbs: 0 g; Fiber: 0 g; Sugar: 0 g

CHEESY BEEF ENCHILADAS

10 minutes   5 minutes   4

INGREDIENTS

- 500 g minced beef
- 1 packet taco seasoning
- 8 medium tortillas
- 150 g grated cheese
- 100 g soured cream
- 1 can of black beans
- 1 can of tomatoes, chopped
- 1 can of chillies, chopped
- 1 can red enchilada sauce
- A handful of cilantro, chopped

DIRECTIONS

1. Take a medium frying pan, brown the beef and add the taco seasoning, combining well
2. Add the beef, beans, tomatoes and chillies to the tortillas, spreading equally
3. Line the Air Fryer with foil and place the tortillas inside
4. Pour your enchilada sauce over the top, sprinkle with cheese
5. Cook at 200°C for 5 minutes
6. Remove from the Air Fryer, add toppings and serve

Nutrition: Calories: 320; Fat: 43 g; Protein: 25 g; Carbs: 25 g; Fiber: 0 g; Sugar: 0 g

LAMB STEAKS

5 minutes | 10 minutes | 4

INGREDIENTS

- 4 Lamb Steaks
- 1 tsp. Frozen Chopped Garlic
- 2 tsp. **Extra Virgin Olive Oil**
- 2 tsp. Lemon Juice
- 2 tsp. **Honey**
- 1 tsp. **Thyme**
- Salt & Pepper
- Fresh Mint

DIRECTIONS

1. Place the lamb steaks on a chopping board, season with salt, pepper and dried thyme.
2. Thinly chop two tablespoons of mint and load into a bowl with everything except the lamb. Mix well then spoon over the lamb steaks. Place the steaks into the fridge for an hour, allow to marinate.
3. Load the steaks into the Air Fryer basket, add extra mint.
4. Air fry 10 minutes, 180°C.

Nutrition: Calories: 274.5; Fat: 19 g; Protein: 21g; Carbs: 4 g; Fiber: 0 g; Sugar: 4 g

MUSTARD GLAZED PORK

2 hours   20 minutes   4

INGREDIENTS

- 750 g pork tenderloin
- 1 tbsp. minced garlic
- ¼ tsp. salt
- Pinch of cracked black pepper
- 3 tbsp. mustard
- 3 tbsp. brown sugar
- 1 tsp. Italian seasoning
- 1 tsp. rosemary

DIRECTIONS

1. Cut slits into the pork and place the minced garlic into the slits.
2. Season with the salt and pepper.
3. Take a mixing bowl and add the remaining ingredients, combining well.
4. Rub the mix over the pork and allow to marinate for 2 hours.
5. Place in the Air Fryer and cook at 200°C for 20 minutes.

Nutrition: Calories: 256; Fat: 5.5 g; Protein: 23 g; Carbs: 8.5 g; Fiber: 0.5 g; Sugar: 7.5 g

PORK CHOPS

10 minutes | 10 minutes | 4

INGREDIENTS

- 4 boneless pork chops
- 2 tbsp. extra-virgin olive oil
- 50 g freshly grated Parmesan
- 1 tsp. salt
- 1 tsp. paprika
- 1 tsp. garlic powder
- 1 tsp. onion powder
- 1/2 tsp. freshly ground black pepper

DIRECTIONS

1. Pat your pork chops dry with some paper towels, then coat both of the sides with oil. Take a medium bowl, mix Parmesan, spices. Coat both of the sides of the pork chops with the Parmesan mixture.
2. Place the pork chops in Air Fryer basket, cook at 190°C for 9 minutes, flipping halfway through.

Nutrition: Calories: 306; Fat: 22 g; Protein: 23 g; Carbs: 1.5 g; Fiber: 0 g; Sugar: 0 g

BEEF KEBOBS

45 minutes   15 minutes   4

INGREDIENTS

- 500g beef, cubed
- 200g low fat sour cream
- 2 tbsp. soy sauce
- 1 bell pepper
- ½ onion, chopped
- 20 x 16 cm skewers

DIRECTIONS

1. Take a medium bowl and combine the sour cream and soy sauce
2. Add the cubed beef and marinate for at least 30 minutes
3. Cut the pepper and onion into 2.5 cm pieces
4. Soak the skewers in warm water for about 10 minutes
5. Place the beef, bell peppers and onion onto the skewers, alternating between each one
6. Cook at 200°C for 10 minutes, flip halfway through.

Nutrition: Calories: 250; Fat: 15 g; Protein: 23g ; Carbs: 4 g; Fiber: 0 g; Sugar: 0 g

MOZZARELLA-STUFFED MEATBALLS

15 minutes   15 minutes   4

INGREDIENTS

- 450 g beef mince
- 50 g bread crumbs
- 25 g freshly grated Parmesan
- 5 g freshly chopped parsley
- 1 large egg
- 2 cloves garlic, crushed
- 1 tsp. dried oregano
- Salt
- Freshly ground black pepper
- 85 g fresh 363, cut into 16 cubes
- Marinara, for serving

DIRECTIONS

1. Take a large bowl, mix beef, parsley, bread crumbs, Parmesan, egg, garlic, oregano. Add salt and pepper.
2. Scoop 2 tablespoons of meat, flatten into a patty in your hand. Arrange a cube of mozzarella in the centre and pinch the meat up around the cheese and roll into a ball. Repeat with remaining meat to make 16 total meatballs.
3. Arrange the meatballs in the Air Fryer basket and cook 190°C, 12 minutes.
4. Serve with warmed marinara.

Nutrition: Calories: 363; Fat: 21.5 g; Protein: 30.5 g; Carbs: 7 g; Fiber: 0 g; Sugar: 0.5 g

HERBED STEAK

30 minutes | 20 minutes | 4

INGREDIENTS

- 4 tbsp. butter, softened
- 2 cloves garlic, crushed
- 2 tsp. freshly chopped parsley
- 1 tsp. freshly chopped chives
- 1 tsp. freshly chopped thyme
- 1 tsp. freshly chopped rosemary
- 1 (900g) bone-in ribeye
- Salt
- Freshly ground black pepper

DIRECTIONS

1. In a small bowl, mix butter, herbs. Arrange in centre of a piece of cling film and roll into a log. Twist ends together to keep tight and refrigerate until hardened, 20 minutes.
2. Add salt and pepper on both sides of the steak.
3. Place steak in the Air Fryer basket and cook, flipping halfway through, 200°C 12-14 minutes for medium, depending on thickness of steak.
4. Top your steak with a slice of herb butter.

Nutrition: Calories: 415; Fat: 22 g; Protein: 51 g; Carbs: 3 g; Fiber: 0 g; Sugar: 0 g

CHAPTER 3: RED MEAT RECIPES

BEEF FRIED RICE

10 minutes | 15 minutes | 3

INGREDIENTS

- 100 g cooked rice
- 500 g beef strips, cooked
- 1 tbsp. sesame oil
- 1 onion, diced
- 1 egg
- 2 tsp. garlic powder
- 1 tbsp. vegetable oil
- 100 g frozen peas
- Salt
- Pepper

DIRECTIONS

1. Preheat Air Fryer to 175°C
2. Add pepper, salt and garlic powder to the beef
3. Cook the beef in a pan until almost done
4. Mix the rice with peas, carrots and vegetable oil, combining well
5. Add the rice mixture to the beef and combine
6. Add to the Air Fryer and cook for about 10 minutes
7. Add the egg and cook until the egg has completely cooked

Nutrition: Calories: 446; Fat: 14 g; Protein: 44 g; Carbs: 31 g; Fiber: 2 g; Sugar: 2 g

CHICKEN PARMESAN

16 minutes — 10 minutes — 4

INGREDIENTS

- 1/2 tsp. garlic powder
- 1/2 tsp. chilli flakes
- 240 g marinara/tomato sauce
- 100 g grated mozzarella
- Freshly chopped parsley, for garnish
- 2 large boneless chicken breasts
- Salt
- 100 g panko bread crumbs
- 25 g freshly grated Parmesan
- 1 tsp. dried oregano
- Freshly ground black pepper
- 40 g plain flour
- 2 large eggs

DIRECTIONS

1. Cut the chicken to create 4 thin pieces. Add salt and pepper on both sides.
2. Prepare dredging station: Place the flour in a shallow bowl, add a large pinch of salt and pepper. Now place the eggs in a second bowl and beat them. Take a third bowl, mix Parmesan, bread crumbs, garlic powder, oregano and chilli flakes.
3. One at a time, coat in flour, then dip in eggs, and finally press both sides into your panko mixture.
4. Arrange the chicken into your Air Fryer basket and cook 5 minutes on each side, 200°C. Top the chicken with sauce, mozzarella and cook 3 minutes more, 200°C, until cheese is melty and golden.
5. Serve with parsley garnish.

Nutrition: Calories: 397; Fat: 18 g; Protein: 30 g; Carbs: 25 g; Fiber: 2.5 g; Sugar: 5 g

SPICY CHICKEN THIGHS

10 minutes · 25 minutes · 4

INGREDIENTS

- 80 ml low-sodium soy sauce
- Thinly sliced spring onions, for garnish
- 2 tbsp. chilli garlic sauce
- Juice of 1 lime
- Toasted sesame seeds, for garnish
- 2 cloves garlic, crushed
- 2 tsp. freshly grated ginger
- 60 ml extra-virgin olive oil
- 2 tbsp. honey
- 4 bone-in, skin-on chicken thighs

DIRECTIONS

1. Take a large bowl, mix oil, soy sauce, honey, garlic, chilli garlic sauce, lime juice, and ginger. Reserve a cup of 120ml of marinade. Add chicken thighs to the bowl and toss to coat. Now cover and refrigerate for 30 minutes or more.
2. Remove 2 of the thighs from the marinade and arrange them in the Air Fryer basket. Cook at 200°C until thighs are reach an internal temperature of 73°C, 15-20 minutes. Now transfer the thighs to a plate, tent with foil. Now repeat with the remaining thighs.
3. Meanwhile, take a small saucepan over medium heat, bring marinade to a boil. Reduce heat, simmer until sauce thickens slightly, 4-5 minutes.
4. Brush the sauce over the thighs, garnish with spring onions and sesame seeds.

Nutrition: Calories: 524; Fat: 48 g; Protein: 10 g; Carbs: 14 g; Fiber: 0.25 g; Sugar: 9 g

CHICKEN BREAST

5 minutes | 15 minutes | 2

INGREDIENTS

- Wax paper or plastic wrap
- 2 skinless/boneless chicken breast halves
- 1 tsp. salt
- 2 tsp. paprika
- 2 tsp. onion powder
- 2 tsp. black pepper
- 1 tsp. white pepper
- 1 tsp. cayenne pepper
- 1 tsp. ground cumin
- 1 tsp. ground oregano

DIRECTIONS

1. Put your chicken breasts between a few sheets of wax paper or plastic wrap and use a meat pounder until the chicken is evenly thick.
2. Make the blackened seasoning by mixing paprika, salt, onion powder, the 3 types of pepper, ground cumin, ground oregano. Check that the spices are well mixed.
3. Dredge the chicken in the seasoning spice mixture.
4. Place the chicken breasts in the Air Fryer basket. Temperature to 145°C, cook for 8 minutes.
5. After 8 minutes, remove the basket, turn the chicken breasts over. Set the temperature to 180°C and cook for 6 more minutes.

Nutrition: Calories: 355.5; Fat: 18.5 g; Protein: 41.5 g; Carbs: 1 g; Fiber: 0 g; Sugar: 0 g

GARLIC HERB TURKEY BREAST

5 minutes | 45 minutes | 6

INGREDIENTS

- 900 g turkey breast, skin on
- Salt
- 1 tsp. freshly chopped rosemary
- Freshly ground black pepper
- 1 tsp. freshly chopped thyme
- 4 tbsp. butter, melted
- 3 cloves garlic, crushed

DIRECTIONS

1. Pat the turkey breast dry and add salt and pepper on both sides.
2. Take a small bowl, mix melted butter, garlic, thyme, and rosemary.
3. Brush the butter all over the turkey breast.
4. Arrange in your Air Fryer basket, skin side up, cook at 190°C (170°C fan), 40 minutes, until internal temperature reaches 73°C, flip halfway through.
5. Let it rest for 5 minutes before slicing.

Nutrition: Calories: 328; Fat: 18 g; Protein: 33 g; Carbs: 5.5 g; Fiber: 0.5 g; Sugar: 0 g

TURKEY AND MUSHROOM BURGERS

10 minutes   10 minutes   2

INGREDIENTS

- 180g mushrooms
- 500g minced turkey
- 1 tsp. garlic powder
- 1 tsp. onion powder
- ½ tsp. salt
- ½ tsp. pepper

DIRECTIONS

1. Take your food processor and add the mushrooms, pulsing into they form a puree. Season and pulse once more
2. Remove from the food processor and tip into a mixing bowl
3. Add the turkey to the bowl and combine well
4. Take a little of the mixture into your hands and shape into burgers. You should be able to make five
5. Spray each burger with a little cooking spray and place in the Air Fryer
6. Cook at 160°C for 10 minutes

Nutrition: Calories: 357.5; Fat: 14 g; Protein: 54 g; Carbs: 0 g; Fiber: 0 g; Sugar: 0 g

CHICKEN STRIPS

< 30 minutes   10-30 minutes   3

INGREDIENTS

- 2 large **garlic** cloves, minced or crushed
- 5 tbsp. plain yogurt
- ¼ tsp. **salt**, plus extra for seasoning
- 2 chicken breasts
- 6 tbsp. plain flour
- 6 tbsp. **panko** breadcrumbs
- 1 tsp. sweet **smoked paprika**
- 1 tsp. **garlic** granules
- ½ tsp. cayenne pepper
- freshly ground black pepper
- 1 free-range egg
- **olive oil** cooking spray

For the creamy honey mustard dip:

- 1 tbsp. runny honey
- 1 tbsp. light **mayonnaise**
- 1 tbsp. Dijon mustard
- ½ tbsp. wholegrain mustard
- ½ tsp. white wine vinegar

DIRECTIONS

1. To marinate the chicken, mix garlic, yoghurt and salt. Cut the chicken into 3cm wide strips, marinate in the yoghurt mixture for 20 minutes or more.
2. Take a medium bowl and mix the flour, paprika, breadcrumbs, cayenne pepper, garlic granules and a good amount of salt and pepper to create dredging mixture. Take another small bowl, beat the egg and add salt, pepper.
3. Shake off any excess yogurt from each of the chicken strip before dipping it first in the egg, then in the dredging mixture. Use different hands for wet and dry ingredients.
4. Spray the bottom of the Air Fryer basket with olive oil spray, arrange a single layer of chicken strips in the bottom. Spray the top of the strips with oil before air-frying 15 minutes, 200°C, turning roughly halfway through. Repeat until all the strips are cooked (work in batches).
5. Meanwhile, mix all the ingredients for the creamy honey mustard dip in a small bowl, set aside.
6. Serve.

Nutrition: Calories: 452; Fat: 15.5 g; Protein: 36 g; Carbs: 38 g; Fiber: 3 g; Sugar: 2.5 g

CHICKEN NUGGETS

20 minutes | 10 minutes | 4

INGREDIENTS
- 500g chicken tenders
- 4 tbsp. salad dressing mix
- 2 tbsp. plain flour
- 1 egg, beaten
- 50g dry bread crumbs

DIRECTIONS
1. Take a large mixing bowl and add the chicken
2. Sprinkle the seasoning over the top and ensure the chicken is evenly coated
3. Allow the chicken to rest for 10 minutes
4. Add the flour into a resealable bag
5. Pour the breadcrumbs onto a medium sized plate
6. Transfer the chicken into the resealable bag and coat with the flour, giving it a good shake
7. Remove the chicken and dip into the egg, and then roll into the breadcrumbs, coating evenly
8. Repeat with the chicken
9. Heat your Air Fryer to 200°C
10. Arrange the chicken inside the fryer and cook for 4 minutes, before turning over and cooking for another 4 minutes
11. Remove and serve whilst hot

Nutrition: Calories: 291.5; Fat: 13 g; Protein: 29 g; Carbs: 11 g; Fiber: 1 g; Sugar: 0.5 g

ROTISSERIE CHICKEN

10 minutes 40 minutes 6

INGREDIENTS

- 2 tsp. of onion powder
- 1 tsp. of smoked paprika
- 1/4 tsp. of cayenne
- 1 (1.3kg.) chicken, into 8 pieces
- 2 tsp. of dried oregano
- Salt
- 2 tsp. of garlic powder
- Freshly ground black pepper
- 1 tbsp. of dried thyme

DIRECTIONS

1. Season all the chicken with salt and pepper. Take a medium bowl, whisk together herbs and spices, then rub the spice mix all over the chicken.
2. Add dark meat pieces to the Air Fryer basket and cook at 180°C, 10 minutes, then flip, cook 10 minutes more. Repeat with the chicken breasts, but reducing time to 16 minutes, 8 per side. Using a meat thermometer, check that the chicken is cooked through, each piece should register 73°C.

Nutrition: Calories: 200; Fat: 5 g; Protein: 35.5 g; Carbs: 0 g; Fiber: 0 g; Sugar: 0 g

CHICKEN TENDERS

10 minutes | 20 minutes | 4

INGREDIENTS

For The Chicken Tenders:
- 675 g chicken tenders
- Salt
- Freshly ground black pepper
- 195 g plain flour
- 250 g panko bread crumbs
- 2 large eggs
- 60 ml buttermilk
- Cooking spray

For The Honey Mustard:
- 80 g mayonnaise
- 3 tbsp. honey
- 2 tbsp. dijon mustard
- 1/4 tsp. hot sauce (optional)
- Pinch of salt
- Freshly ground black pepperw

DIRECTIONS

1. Season the chicken tenders with some salt and some black pepper on both sides. Place flour, bread crumbs in two separate shallow bowls. Whisk eggs and buttermilk in a third bowl. Dip chicken in flour, one at a time, then egg mixture, and in bread crumbs, pressing to coat.
2. Place the chicken tenders in your Air Fryer basket, do not overcrowd it. Spray the tops with cooking spray, cook at 200°C, 5 minutes. Flip the chicken over, spray the tops with more cooking spray, cook another 5 minutes. Repeat with the remaining chicken tenders.
3. Make the sauce: Take a small bowl, whisk together honey, mayonnaise, dijon, and hot sauce (optional). Add salt and a few cracks of black pepper.
4. Serve with honey mustard.

Nutrition: Calories: 720; Fat: 21 g; Protein: 55 g; Carbs: 74 g; Fiber: 7 g; Sugar: 11 g

CHAPTER 2: POULTRY RECIPES

CHICKEN WINGS WITH HONEY AND SESAME

< 30 minutes   10-30 minutes   1-2

INGREDIENTS

- 450-500g chicken wings with tips removed
- 1 tbsp. olive oil
- 3 tbsp. cornflour
- 1 tbsp. runny honey
- 1 tsp. soy sauce or tamari
- 1 tsp. rice wine vinegar
- 1 tsp. toasted sesame oil
- 2 tsp. sesame seeds, toasted
- 1 large spring onion, thinly sliced
- salt and freshly ground black pepper

DIRECTIONS

1. Take a large bowl, toss together chicken wings, olive oil and a generous amount of salt and black pepper.
2. Toss in the cornflour, one tablespoon at a time, until the wings are well coated.
3. Air-fry the chicken wings in a single layer for 25 minutes, 180°C, turning halfway through.
4. Meanwhile, in a large bowl, make the glaze by whisking together the soy sauce, honey, rice, wine vinegar and toasted sesame oil.
5. Now tip the cooked wings into the glaze, tossing until coated. Place them in the Air Fryer in a single layer for another 5 minutes.
6. Toss the wings in the remaining glaze. Now sprinkle with the toasted sesame seeds and the spring onion.
7. Serve.

Nutrition: Calories: 544; Fat: 32.5 g; Protein: 37.5g; Carbs: 23.5 g; Fiber: 2 g; Sugar: 9 g

FRENCH TOAST STICKS

5 minutes | 10 minutes | 6

INGREDIENTS
- 3 tbsp. of caster sugar
- Salt
- 80 ml of double cream
- 1/4 tsp. of ground cinnamon
- 1/2 tsp. of vanilla extract
- 6 thick slices white loaf or brioche, each slice cut into thirds
- Maple syrup, for serving
- 2 large eggs
- 80 ml of whole milk

DIRECTIONS
1. Take a large shallow baking dish and beat sugar, cream, eggs, cinnamon, vanilla, milk, and a pinch of salt.
2. Add bread, turn to coat for few times.
3. Arrange the french toast into the Air Fryer basket, working in batches to not overcrowd the basket. Set Air Fryer to 190°C, cook until golden, about 8 minutes, tossing halfway through.
4. Serve warm, drizzled with maple syrup.

Nutrition: Calories: 166; Fat: 7 g; Protein: 6 g; Carbs: 18 g; Fiber: 2.5 g; Sugar: 7 g

CHEESE OMELETTE

10 minutes | 10 minutes | 1

INGREDIENTS

- 2 eggs
- 150 ml milk
- Pinch of salt
- 40g shredded cheese
- Any toppings you like, such as mushrooms, peppers, onions, etc

DIRECTIONS

1. In a medium mixing jug, combine the eggs and milk
2. Add the salt and garnishes and combine well
3. Take a 15x8 cm pan and grease well, before pouring the mixture inside
4. Arrange the pan inside the Air Fryer basket
5. Cook at 170°C for 10 minutes
6. At the halfway point, sprinkle the cheese on top and loosen the edges with a spatula
7. Remove and enjoy!

Nutrition: Calories: 395; Fat: 27 g; Protein: 25 g; Carbs: 7 g; Fiber: 0 g; Sugar: 6 g

SAUSAGE SANDWICHES

11 minutes   15 minutes   4

INGREDIENTS

- 4 breakfast sausage patties
- 4 eggs
- kosher salt, pepper
- 1 tbsp. butter
- 4 bagel thins or english muffins
- 4 slices cheese of choice

DIRECTIONS

1. Lay the breakfast sausage patties in your Air Fryer basket. Set the Air Fryer to 200°C, 15 minutes.
2. Remove the sausage and lay on some paper towels to drain the excess fat.
3. Take a bowl and beat the eggs inside, add kosher salt and pepper. In a medium size skillet, medium low heat, add butter, once it's melted add beaten eggs in a single layer.
4. Cook 2-3 minutes and flip, cook one or two more minutes. Remove the eggs from the pan, cut into 4 equal pieces.
5. Lay the bottom part of the English muffin or the bagel in the Air Fryer basket. Add a sausage patty to each, top with the cooked egg and a slice of cheese.
6. Put the top of the english muffin or the bagel on each sandwich.
7. Set the Air Fryer to 200°C, 4 to 5 minutes.
8. Serve.

Nutrition: Calories: 323; Fat: 13 g; Protein: 22 g; Carbs: 29 g; Fiber: 4 g; Sugar: 1 g

VEGETABLE FRITTATA

5 minutes | 10 minutes | 1 Frittata

INGREDIENTS

- Oil or butter to grease the pan
- 3 eggs
- 1/4 red pepper, diced
- 1/4 green pepper, diced
- 10 baby spinach leaves, chopped
- Handful of cheddar cheese, grated
- Salt and pepper to season, optional

DIRECTIONS

1. Take a bowl and beat the eggs inside. Season with salt and pepper (optional).
2. Grease the pan with the oil or butter and place it in the Air Fryer. Switch to 180°C, allow to heat up for a minute. Add the peppers, cook for 3 minutes.
3. Pour the spinach and egg mix in. Sprinkle grated cheese across the top. Cook for another 6 minutes, checking to make sure it isn't over cooking.

Nutrition: Calories: 514; Fat: 31 g; Protein: 38 g; Carbs: 18 g; Fiber: 8 g; Sugar: 3 g

CHOCOLATE CHIP COOKIES

10 minutes   15 minutes   12

INGREDIENTS

- 115 g butter, melted
- 55 g brown sugar
- 50 g caster sugar
- 1 large egg
- 1 tsp. pure vanilla extract
- 185 g plain flour
- 1/2 tsp. bicarbonate of soda
- 1/2 tsp. salt
- 120 g chocolate chips
- 35 g chopped walnuts

DIRECTIONS

1. Take medium bowl and whisk together melted butter and sugars.
2. Add egg and vanilla, whisk until incorporated.
3. Add salt, flour, bicarbonate of soda and stir.
4. Arrange a small piece of parchment in the Air Fryer's basket, making sure there is air flow around the edges.
5. Work in batches, using a large cookie scoop and scoop dough onto parchment, about 3 tablespoons, leaving 5cm between each of them, press to flatten slightly.
6. Bake in the Air Fryer at 180°C for 8 minutes. Cookies will be golden and slightly soft. Let them cool 5 minutes before serving.

Nutrition: Calories: 224; Fat: 13 g; Protein: 3.5 g; Carbs: 24 g; Fiber: 2 g; Sugar: 12 g

BACON MUFFINS

7 minutes | 6 minutes | 1

INGREDIENTS

- 1 Large Egg
- 1 Slice of Unsmoked Bacon
- 1 English All Butter Muffin
- 2 Slices of Burger Cheese
- 1 Pinch of Salt and Pepper

DIRECTIONS

1. Crack the large egg into either a ramekin or oven proof dish
2. Slice the muffin in half
3. Layer 1 slice of burger cheese on 1 half
4. Place now the muffin and bacon in the Air Fryer drawer, place the ovenproof dish or ramekin in the drawer too.
5. Heat up the Air Fryer to 200°C for 6 minutes
6. Once is done, assemble the breakfast muffin and add the extra slice of cheese on top.

Nutrition: Calories: 291; Fat: 12 g; Protein: 15 g; Carbs: 25 g; Fiber: 2 g; Sugar: 0 g

PATATAS BRAVAS

10 minutes   25 minutes   4

INGREDIENTS

- 300g potatoes, cut into chunks
- 1 tbsp. avocado oil
- 1 tsp. garlic powder
- Pinch of salt
- Pinch of pepper
- 1 tbsp. smoked paprika

DIRECTIONS

1. Take a large saucepan of water and bring to boil, add potatoes, cooking for 6 minutes
2. Strain your potatoes, place them on a piece of kitchen towel, once a little cool, pat dry
3. Leave the potatoes to arrive at room temperate
4. Take a large mixing bowl and add the garlic powder, salt, and pepper and add the avocado oil, mixing
5. Add now your potatoes to the bowl and coat liberally
6. Place the potatoes into the basket and arrange them with space in-between
7. Set your fryer to 200°C
8. Cook the potatoes for 15 minutes, giving them a shake at the halfway point
9. Remove and serve

Nutrition: Calories: 88.5; Fat: 3.5 g; Protein: 1.5 g; Carbs: 13 g; Fiber: 1.5 g; Sugar: 0.5 g

FRIED BACON

10 minutes   10 minutes   2

INGREDIENTS

- 4-5 rashers of lean bacon, fat cut off

DIRECTIONS

1. Line up the Air Fryer basket with parchment paper, to soak up excess grease
2. Arrange your bacon in the basket, ensuring you don't overcrowd; around 4-5 slices should be enough, depending upon the size of your machine
3. Set the fryer to 200°C
4. Cook for 10 minutes for crispy, and an extra 2 if you want it super-crispy
5. Serve and enjoy!

Nutrition: Calories: 161; Fat: 12 g; Protein: 12 g; Carbs: 0.5 g; Fiber: 0 g; Sugar: 0 g

EGG & HAM CUPS

14 minutes   20 minutes   4

INGREDIENTS

- 4 eggs
- 8 slices of bread, pre-toasted
- 2 slices of ham
- A pinch of salt
- A pinch of pepper
- A little extra butter for greasing

DIRECTIONS

1. Take 4 ramekins and brush them with butter to grease the inside
2. Take the slices of bread and flatten them down with a rolling pin
3. Arrange the toast inside the ramekins, rolling it around the sides, with 2 slices in each ramekin
4. Line the inside of each ramekin with a slice of ham
5. Crack one egg into each ramekin
6. Season with a little salt and pepper
7. Place now the ramekins into your Air Fryer and cook at 160°C for 15 minutes
8. Remove from the fryer and wait to cool just slightly
9. Remove from the ramekins and serve

Nutrition: Calories: 204; Fat: 6 g; Protein: 12 g; Carbs: 24 g; Fiber: 5 g; Sugar: 3 g

CHAPTER 1: BREAKFAST RECIPES

SWEET POTATO HASH

15 minutes   45 minutes   3

INGREDIENTS

- 2 sweet potatoes, cubed
- 2 slices of bacon, small cubes
- 2 tbsp. olive oil
- 1 tbsp. smoked paprika
- 1 tsp. salt
- 1 tsp. black pepper (ground)
- 1 tsp. dill weed (dried)

DIRECTIONS

1. Preheat your Air Fryer to 200°C
2. Take a large bowl and add the olive oil
3. Add the potatoes, bacon, salt, pepper, dill, and paprika into the bowl and toss to evenly coat
4. Pour now the contents of the bowl into your Air Fryer and cook for 12-16 minutes, stir halfway through.
5. Serve.

Nutrition: Calories: 204; Fat: 6 g; Protein: 12 g; Carbs: 24 g; Fiber: 5 g; Sugar: 3 g

to remove both the drawer and the basket.

- Finally, wipe the outside of your Air Fryer with a damp cloth or a sponge.

If there are any odors that seem to be stuck to your Air Fryer after cooking a strong food, even after you have cleaned it, then you can consider using a product called NewAir.

Just soak it in with water for about 3o minutes to an hour before you clean it. If the smell remains, then rub one lemon half over the drawer and the basket. Allow it to soak for another 30 minutes before washing it again.

Please do be careful with any non-stick appliances. They are a wonder for cleaning, but they can flake or come off over time. Be gentle, as you do not want anything to scratch or to even chip the coating. Not only does it ruin a little bit of the aesthetic look, a small part of your Air Fryer will constantly be struggling with sticky food.

There you have it! The first stepping stones and foundational knowledge of an Air Fryer. The device you will choose, and how you will use it is up to you, but there are still so many exciting varieties, choices, and options to come!

SILICONE BAKING CUPS

From egg bites to muffins, these are individual cups you can use in order to help compensate for the smaller space within an Air Fryer. The silicone material is heat-resistant, and allows for easier release of the contents, which spares you a lot of time cleaning. If you are a fan of baking, then this is a must have.

OIL SPRAYER

Naturally, one of the top benefits is needing much less oil when cooking with an Air Fryer, but it does not necessarily mean that you can cook with no oil at all. An oil sprayer is the key to getting the food you want to that nice golden-brown. You can use any oil that you like to use when cooking; all you need is a little spritz before you close the machine, and you are set!

THERMAPEN

Having the right cooking time is very important, but temperature also counts for a lot, and this is a nice little accessory to add to your collection. Having an instant-read thermometer can ensure all the food you have is cooked (and evenly so). If you are not completely certain at what temperatures food should be, you can always check out the various different guides.

HOW TO CLEAN AN AIR FRYER

As mentioned before, an Air Fryer is really easy to clean, but that doesn't mean you'll never need to clean it! Also, please remember that the cleanliness of your machine depends on how often you use it, and what you use it for.

It is recommended that you clean your Air Fryer after every use. As tempting as it may be to skip a day, it really is not worth it over the long run.

And that is the first step that comes with cleaning an Air Fryer:

- Do not delay the cleaning. Simply don't. Allowing crumbs or random bits of food to harden overnight can turn an easy task into a nightmare of a chore. If you do happen to air-fry foods that come with a form of sticky sauce, then the warmer they are, the easier again they will be to clean and remove.

- Unplug the machine, and use warm and soapy water to properly remove the dirt and components. You do not want anything abrasive in there. If there is food that gets stuck, try soaking it until it is soft enough to remove.

- If there is any food that happens to be stuck on the grate or in the basket, then you should consider gently using a toothpick or even a wooden skewer to scrape it off, in order to be thorough with your cleaning process.

- Remember to wipe the inside with a damp, soapy cloth, and remember convenience, then this is the Air Fryer to go for.

ACCESSORY TOOLS FOR AIR FRYER COOKING

I love how Air Fryers save time, so I've compiled a list of my favorite time-saving tools that I often use when meal prepping with my Air Fryer. Anything to help make your life easier and healthier should certainly be considered, and what better way to help than by adding some accessories to your Air Fryer inventory?

MANDOLINE

Preparation is always needed before jumping into air frying, and getting yourself the mandoline slicer is the perfect tool to slice online rings, pickles, or even the best and crunchiest chips. You can select the thickness or thinness, depending on what the recipe needs and says, so you will always be able to get the perfect crispness.

GRILL PAN

This is simply a pan created with a perforated surface. With this tool, you can both grill and sear foods like fish or even vegetables inside your Air Fryer. They are also commonly non-stick, which really helps your overall cleanup.

However, before you purchase a grill pan, make sure the Air Fryer model you have does support the grill pan. The last thing you want is to find that your grill pan just does not fit inside your Air Fryer.

HEAT RESISTANT TONGS

There is no denying how hot an Air Fryer can get inside, and unless you are a superhero, you will need some help maneuvering in foods in and outside of the basket if need be. Using heat-resistant tongs can really make your life infinitely easier by keeping your foods, and your hands, safe. They are affordable, and really useful to allow for an even cooking process.

AIR FRYER LINERS

If you'd like to further decrease your clean-up time, then this is for you! These liners are both non-stick and non-toxic, making this a classic little investment for you to consider. They prevent the food from sticking to your Air Fryer and help in the process of keeping your little machine clean. You will not have to worry about burnt foods inside your fryer again!

AIR FRYER RACK

This adds a little bit more versatility as you can really take advantage of the surface cooking. With a rack, you ensure that heat is evenly distributed to all 360 degrees of your food. They are very safe and easy to use, and they increase the number of dishes you can cook at the same time

BAKING PANS

With an Air Fryer, you can even bake! You just need the right equipment, such as a barrel or round pan. With this you can even bake pizza, bread, muffins, and more. Imagine telling people you baked your own cake with an Air Fryer!

TWO COMMON DIFFERENCES

Beyond those functional differences, there are two mainstream designs of Air Fryers: basket Air Fryers and oven Air Fryers. Each has very unique and distinguished features in which to enjoy. Let us take a look at the differences between the two:

BASKET AIR FRYERS

Basket fryers are known to need less space than oven Air Fryers, which is very practical if you have limited space. Not only does it save space, but it also saves time, as the food is quickly heated up (without unnecessarily heating up the kitchen). Unlike an oven Air Fryer, and the larger traditional oven, it only takes about 1-2 minutes for the basket Air Fryer to heat up, and it is quite easy to place the foods inside of the basket.

The cons are, for one, that it does make a lot more noise than the oven Air Fryer. You also will not be able to watch the food as it cooks, which can increase the chances of burnt food if you are not careful. Also, a basket Air Fryer may not be the best if you need to cook a lot of food, as it is limited in capacity. This means that batch cooking may be required if you need a large amount of food.

This makes a basket Air Fryer ideal if you have a limited budget, don't need to cook a huge amount of food, and have limited free time. They are quick, small, and convenient, especially perfect for people who are students or single working professionals, and maybe even you!

OVEN AIR FRYERS

Oven Air Fryers, in contrast, have a larger capacity, which means you can cook a lot more food at the same time. They also have multiple functions for cooking and cut down on the noise than the basket Air Fryer. You will also be able to move the food closer or even further away from the heating element. There is a lot more flexibility involved in the use of an oven Air Fryer. Best of all, you can place parts of the oven Air Fryer into the dishwasher to be washed (thus cutting down the cleaning process, if you happen to have a dishwasher).

But, do be aware that it takes up more counter space, and takes a larger initial bite out of your wallet. It may also heat up the kitchen more, and if you are in fashion and aesthetic design, it might be disappointing to find out the colors and themes are more limited than basket Air Fryers.

These are the two main common types of Air Fryers; however, there are new types of Air Fryers that are coming to light for you to use and enjoy, most notably, the paddle-type Air Fryer. This version has a paddle that moves through the basket of your Air Fryer in order to help circulate hot air in between each piece of food.

This saves you the effort of pulling your food out at a specific time and shaking or stirring it. These can also be noisy, and heat up the space, and are not small and convenient; however, if you are someone looking for methods of cooking foods that are meant to be deep fried (like chicken tenders). No one really enjoys mushy food. The Air Fryer keeps that desired element while remaining healthy.

All you will really need is just some cooking oil sprayed outside of your food to end up with a cooked interior and a crunchy exterior. So no worries! You still can eat your foods with a crunch and a healthier result!

VERSATILE

Unlike rice cookers meant just for rice, or bread makers meant just for bread, you will find that an Air Fryer leaves a lot of room to be both versatile and healthier. You can cook almost anything you would like in the Air Fryer (as long as it fits). From spaghetti squash, to desserts, even to fried chicken! You will probably never run out of air frying options!

VARIOUS TYPES OF AIR FRYERS AND HOW TO CHOOSE THE ONE FOR YOU

There isn't one standardized choice of Air Fryers, which means you are far more likely to find an Air Fryer that really suits your particular needs. Whether it be size or price, you have a wider variety of choices than what normally comes with conventional ovens.

So what are the key aspects that you need to take into consideration when getting yourself a nice Air Fryer? Let's begin:

- **Dimensions:** Obviously they come in different sizes, and despite saving space, some can still be bulky. When thinking about your countertop, you do want to consider its size and dimensions. You don't want to play a game of tilt with your Air Fryer, nor have it taken up all the extra space you have!

- **Safety Features:** You may want to check that it has an auto shutoff, as it is certainly a desirable feature. Air Fryers can get very hot during use, and an auto-shutoff can save you a lot of stress and fire emergencies. Furthermore, having a cool exterior can prevent potential red and burnt hands. So do yourself a favor and make sure they have all these elements at hand.

- **Reviews:** Naturally, this is the best thing to check out. Considering that the businesses rarely give out all the information, you will certainly find it out when people leave reviews. The customer hides nothing, and if they are unhappy, they make sure everyone else knows about it. However, if people are very happy, many of them will also note it in the reviews, and it is best to target the Air Fryers that tend to have the high reviews.

LOW OPERATING COSTS

Considering how much cooking oil costs these days and the amount you need to use, you will soon be cutting costs in making deep fried foods. All an Air Fryer uses is a small amount of oil and some of the electricity to power up the Air Fryer, about the same amount that a countertop oven would.

Not only will you be cutting out the massive oil costs, which will save money, you will likely also save money by ordering out less, as you'll be able to replicate your favorite foods quickly and easily at home!

NO OIL SMELL

In reality, smelling like the food you just ate is not impressive, regardless of how delicious the food may be. This is what often happens, however, when people enjoy deep fried foods.

When deep frying foods, it also causes the whole house to smell, and as the oil splatters around, it can leave a massive mess. The oil can even harden on the walls, causing grime to build up into a nasty concentration of dirt and grease.

With less cooking oil, Air Fryers don't have any of those oil smells and keeps the space cleaner around you, as all the oils, smells, and actual cooking are contained within the machine.

PRESERVES NUTRIENTS

When you are cooking your food in an Air Fryer, it actually protects a lot of the food from losing all its moisture. This means that with the use of a little oil, as well as circulation with hot air, it can allow your food to keep most of its nutrients which is excellent for you!

If you want to cook healthy foods with the purpose of maintaining as many nutrients as possible, then an Air Fryer is perfect for you!

EASIER TO CLEAN

Cleaning is perhaps the bane of my existence, especially after cooking and having a long day. This can really take away a lot of the pleasure of making yourself a great meal. But an Air Fryer lightens the burden by being easy to clean!

Consistent cleaning after using it (much like any pot or pan) can allow for easier and simpler living. You just need some soapy water and a non-scratch sponge to clean both the exterior and the interior of your Air Fryer. Some Air Fryers are even dishwasher-safe!

GREAT FLAVOUR

The flavor of Air Fryer "fried" foods is nearly identical to traditional frying, and the texture is exact. You can cook a lot of those great frozen foods, such as onion rings or french fries, and still achieve that crunchy effect. This certainly can help you turn to healthier foods, especially if your goal is for healthy but quality meals.

The Air Fryer helps to cook your food to perfect crispness, instead of the soggy mess that happens when you try alternative to make sure it does get evenly crispy. All in all, however, there is no denying the amount of oils is a whole lot less.

This singular change makes all the difference in the world. Healthy eating has never been easier, as you'll get the same crispy and flavorsome results, with minimal amounts of added oils. You'll even be able to "fry" foods you never were able to before—the possibilities are endless!

SAFER AND EASIER

Nothing scares me more than a hot pot of oil. It is an accident waiting to happen, and getting struck with burning oil splatters is no joke! But this, and its corresponding injuries, is often the price to pay for deep fried foods.

Air Fryers are also user-friendly, and this makes a huge difference. You don't have to feel like you are studying for a degree when working with an Air Fryer. Making dinner is far less complicated in an Air Fryer than many of the traditional methods of cooking. For some meals—unless you choose one of the more complex recipes I'll share later—you can even revert to placing a small piece of meat (even if it happens to be frozen!) into the basket and select the cooking settings.

The simplicity of the Air Fryer is its beauty. You will save countless time and unnecessary frustrations, and still make delicious food!

FASTER THAN COOKING IN THE OVEN

Once you buy an Air Fryer and set it to heat for the first time, you won't know what hit you! The average normal oven needs about 10 minutes to preheat. Due to the Air Fryer's smaller size and innovative design, it will be ready to go in no time!

It's even faster during the actual cooking. With the circulation that allows your food to be cooked crisp and even, it cuts a whole lot of cooking time out of the equation. This is amazing, especially in this day and age where technology, work, friends, family, and even pets are constantly demanding our attention.

Just imagine! You could set your food in the Air Fryer, and (with some recipes) it will be ready to eat in less than 20 minutes!

SAVES SPACE

If you are someone living in a small apartment, or a student accommodation, then an Air Fryer is perfect for you. Air Fryers are much smaller in comparison to a conventional oven and you can easily make use of this Air Fryer in 1 cubic foot of your kitchen.

You can even pack your Air Fryer away after use if need be, but the majority of people choose to keep it out on the counter. But it's nice to have the option to move your Air Fryer around if space becomes an issue.

INTRODUCTION

Air Fryers have started to become popular, due to the fact that you can avoid many of the unhealthy aspects of modern cooking. But what is an Air Fryer exactly, and how on earth does it work?

Air Fryers are basically an upgraded, enhanced countertop oven, but they became popular for one particular reason. In fact, many of the manufacturers, such as Philips, market this machine solely based on the claim that the Air Fryers accurately mimic deep-frying, which, although extremely unhealthy, is still very popular in this day and age (as it is, in my opinion, one of the most delicious ways to eat food).

Air Fryers work with the use of a fan and a heating mechanism. You place the food you want cooked in a basket or on the rack, turn on the machine, and the Air Fryer distributes oven-temperature hot air around your food. It provides consistent, pervasive heat evenly to all the food within. This heat circulation achieves the crispy taste and texture that is so tantalizing in deep fried foods, but without the unhealthy and dangerous oil! Both have been replaced by this miracle machine with hot air and a fan.

ADVANTAGES TO USING AN AIR FRYER

I may have already slipped in a few of the advantages to using an Air Fryer, but now let's expand a little more on everything an Air Fryer can do for you. After all, no investment should be made unless it's absolutely worthwhile.

And in truth, the Air Fryer is very worthwhile. I cannot begin to tell you how the advantages start piling up; this is not just another average appliance that everyone is getting because of a simple trend. People are getting Air Fryers because of their incredible, numerous, multifaceted benefits.

There are, however, a few notable advantages of using an Air Fryer, which I'll list below. If you don't know anything else about Air Fryers, I hope that these will convince you of their worth.

HEALTHIER COOKING

This is perhaps the top benefit that comes with air frying. In a society that really struggles with healthy cooking, we can use all the help we can get. Luckily, Air Fryers make it easy, all while maintaining many of the factors that make unhealthy food delicious!
Air Fryers use very little oil, which is one of the best ways to replace those unhealthy fried foods, like fried chicken, potatoes, and so many others. If you are like me (a lover of deep fried foods) then this is the answer to your dilemma of healthy eating while still enjoying the crispy taste of food!

Do keep in mind that you still need to spray fried foods, such as fish, with a touch of oil

Chapter 5: Side Dish Recipes 55
Garlic Cauliflower 55
Fried Chips 56
Broccoli with Oil 57
Courgette Sticks 58
Mozzarella Sticks 59
Roast Potatoes 60
Fried Pickles 61
Aubergine Sticks 62
Brussels Sprouts 63
Green Beans 64

Chapter 6: Dessert Recipes 65
British Victoria Sponge 65
Creamy Chocolate Eclairs 66
Apple Chips 67
Lemon Biscuits 68
Soft Chocolate Brownies 69
Fruit Crumble 70
Mini Apple Pie 71
Shortbread Chocolate Balls 72
Strawberry Cupcakes 73

Index 74
Credits 76

Turkey And Mushroom Burgers *30*
Garlic Herb Turkey Breast *31*
Chicken Breast *32*
Spicy Chicken Thighs *33*
Chicken Parmesan *34*

Chapter 3: Red Meat Recipes 35

Beef Fried Rice *35*
Herbed Steak *36*
Mozzarella-Stuffed Meatballs *37*
Beef Kebobs *38*
Pork Chops *39*
Mustard Glazed Pork *40*
Lamb Steaks *41*
Cheesy Beef Enchiladas *42*
Simple Hamburgers *43*
Beef Wellington *44*

Chapter 4: Fish and Seafood Recipes 45

Beef Wellington *45*
Coconut Prawns *46*
Crab Cakes *47*
Tilapia Fillets *48*
Fish Tacos *49*
Peppery Lemon Shrimp *50*
Tuna Patties *51*
Fried Cod *52*
Sriracha With Salmon *53*
Baked Crunchy Cod *54*

TABLE OF CONTENTS

Table of Contents 4

Introduction 7

Advantages to Using an Air Fryer 7

Various Types of Air Fryers and How to Choose the One for You 10

Two Common Differences 11

Accessory Tools for Air Fryer Cooking 12

How To Clean An Air Fryer 13

Chapter 1: Breakfast Recipes 15

Sweet Potato Hash 15

Egg & Ham Cups 16

Fried Bacon 17

Patatas Bravas 18

Bacon Muffins 19

Chocolate Chip Cookies 20

Vegetable Frittata 21

Sausage Sandwiches 22

Cheese Omelette 23

French Toast Sticks 24

Chapter 2: Poultry Recipes 25

Chicken Wings with Honey and Sesame 25

Chicken Tenders 26

Rotisserie Chicken 27

Chicken Nuggets 28

Chicken Strips 29

Copyright 2022 by Emily Ward - All rights reserved.

The following Book is reproduced below with the goal of providing information that is as accurate and reliable as possible. Regardless, purchasing this Book can be seen as consent to the fact that both the publisher and the author of this book are in no way experts on the topics discussed within and that any recommendations or suggestions that are made herein are for entertainment purposes only. Professionals should be consulted as needed prior to undertaking any of the action endorsed herein.

This declaration is deemed fair and valid by both the American Bar Association and the Committee of Publishers Association and is legally binding throughout the United States.

Furthermore, the transmission, duplication, or reproduction of any of the following work including specific information will be considered an illegal act irrespective of if it is done electronically or in print. This extends to creating a secondary or tertiary copy of the work or a recorded copy and is only allowed with the express written consent from the Publisher. All additional right reserved.

The information in the following pages is broadly considered a truthful and accurate account of facts and as such, any inattention, use, or misuse of the information in question by the reader will render any resulting actions solely under their purview. There are no scenarios in which the publisher or the original author of this work can be in any fashion deemed liable for any hardship or damages that may befall them after undertaking information described herein.

Additionally, the information in the following pages is intended only for informational purposes and should thus be thought of as universal. As befitting its nature, it is presented without assurance regarding its prolonged validity or interim quality. Trademarks that are mentioned are done without written consent and can in no way be considered an endorsement from the trademark holder.

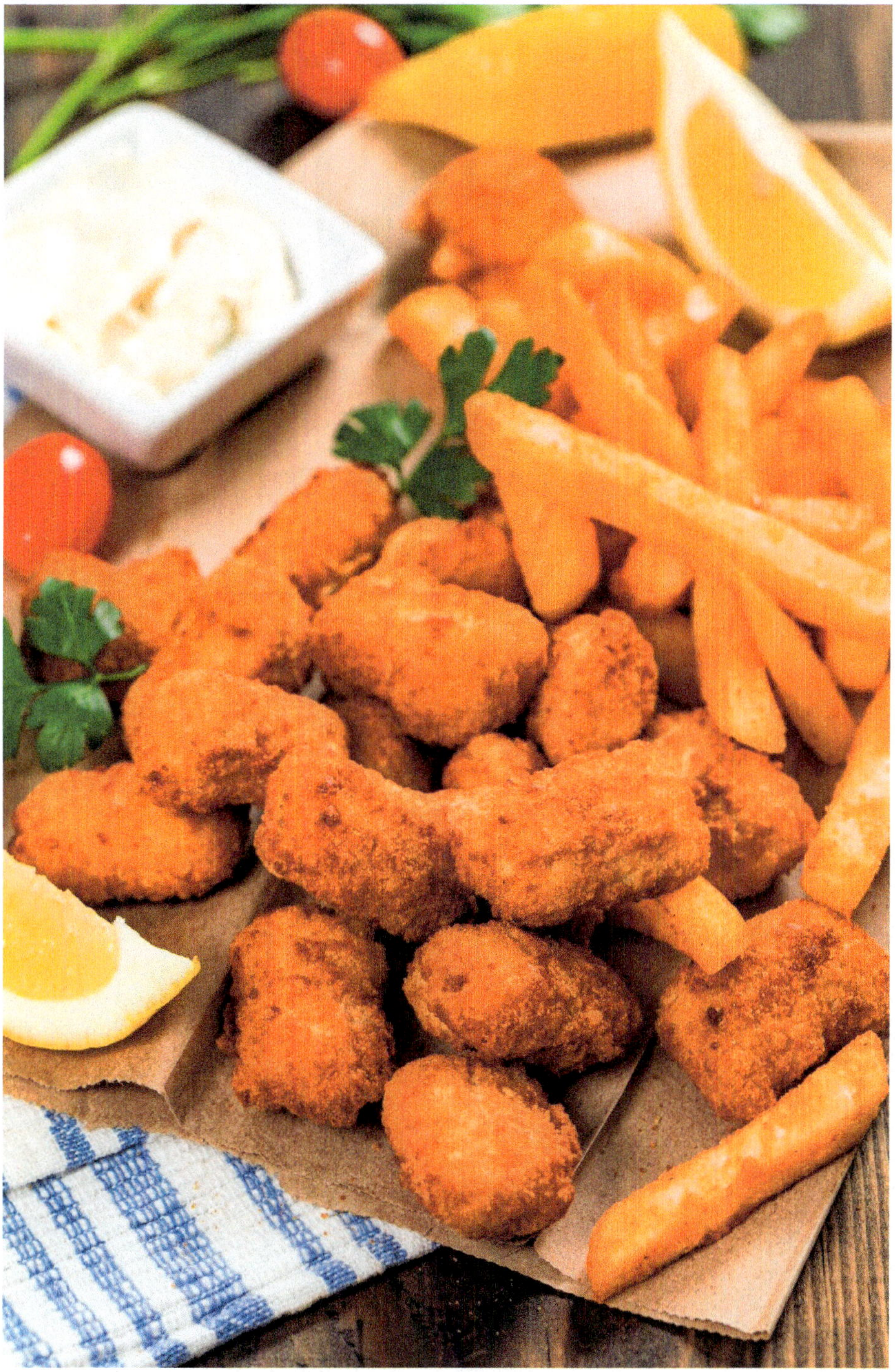

Air Fryer Cookbook UK

Easy and Mouthwatering Recipes with
<u>Colored Pictures</u>

By Emily Ward